I0813614

The Children's Bible

The Children's Bible

ARCTURUS

This edition published in 2025 by Arcturus Publishing Limited
26/27 Bickels Yard, 151–153 Bermondsey Street,
London SE1 3HA

Created by Q2A Media
Edited by Fiona Tulloch, Tracey Kelly, and Frances Evans
Cover design by Peter Ridley

ISBN: 978-1-3988-6188-6
CH004727NT
Supplier 26, Date 0625, PI 00011513

Printed in China

Contents

Introduction

The Bible is the holy book of Christianity. It teaches us the importance of having faith in God and Jesus and how to live a good and decent life in the way that God wants us to. It also tells us how to avoid the temptations of the Devil.

Bible stories can be enjoyed by everyone, whether or not they are Christians. Everyone can learn from the wisdom and teachings it contains.

The Bible is divided into two parts – the Old Testament and the New Testament. The Old Testament tells us how God created the Earth and all the creatures that live on it. It gives us the history of the Jewish people up to a few centuries before the birth of Jesus. The New Testament tells us about the life and preachings of Jesus, about his death and resurrection, and about the early days of the Christian church. (You can read more about the New Testament on page 140).

The Old Testament was originally written in Hebrew and consists of 39 separate books. The first five books are associated with Moses, the great Israelite leader who led his people out of captivity in Egypt to the Promised Land of Canaan.

The Old Testament story begins, however, long before the time of Moses with the first human beings, Adam and Eve. It continues through the lives of the ancestors of the Israelites, such as Noah, Abraham, Isaac, Jacob, and Joseph.

After the five books of Moses come the books of history, which continue the story of the Jewish people up to the third century before Jesus' birth. Here, we meet famous Israelite kings, such as Saul, David, and Solomon, and heroes such as Gideon and Samson.

Following the history books, we have the Psalms and the Song of Solomon, which are books of poetry and songs, and Job, Proverbs, and Ecclesiastes, which are books of wisdom and advice for people.

Finally, we have 17 books containing the words of the great prophets, such as Amos, Isaiah, and Jeremiah, who spoke the words that God gave them to take to the people of Israel and Judah. God wanted to assure his people of his constant love for them and also to warn of what would happen to them if they did not change their bad ways. God also promised to send them the Messiah, which he did – this was Jesus.

Map of Bible Lands

Black Sea
Caspian Sea
MT. ARARAT
BITHYNIA AND PONTUS
ALATIA
CAPPADOCIA
CILICIA
Tarsus
Antioch
Nineveh
ASSYRIA
Tigris River
SYRIA
YPRUS
Sidon
Damascus
BABYLONIA
ea of
alilee
Tyre
Euphrates River
ISRAEL
azareth
Babylon
ericho
Jordan River
Bethlehem
Jerusalem
Dead Sea
JUDEA
Persian Gulf
SINAI
Red Sea

The Creation

Genesis 1:26 Then God said, "And now we will make human beings; they will be like us and resemble us. They will have power over the fish, the birds, and all the animals, domestic and wild, large and small."

In the beginning, the world was covered in water, and everything was dark. The Spirit of God moved over the water.

One day, God said, "Let there be light!" and the Earth was filled with light. God was pleased with this and called the light "day" and the darkness "night." Evening passed and then morning came – this was the very first day.

Then God said, "Let there be a space above the oceans, to separate the heavens from the earth." God named this space "sky." Again, there was evening and morning - this was the second day.

On the third day, God said, "Let dry ground appear from the waters." He named the dry ground "land," and the waters He named "seas." Pleased with what He saw, God commanded, "Let the land produce plants and crops and fruit trees of every kind." The land filled with beautiful trees and plants.

The next day, God commanded, "Let lights appear in the sky to separate day from night, to mark the days, the seasons, and the passing of the years." And it was done. God named the two larger lights the "sun" to rule over the day, and the "moon" to rule over the night, separating light from darkness. Evening passed and morning came, marking the end of the fourth day.

God said, "Let the waters be filled with all kinds of living creatures, and let the air be filled with birds." Knowing that all He had made was good, God blessed the creatures and told them to go and make the skies and water their new homes. Evening passed and morning came, and that was the fifth day.

The next day, God said, "Let the earth produce many kinds of animal life, tame and wild, large and small." And He was pleased with what He saw.

"Now I shall make human beings in my image," said God. "They will rule the earth and the other creatures." God created a man in His image - He called him Adam. Blessing him, God said, "Look after everything I have created. I have provided you with everything you could ever need." Evening passed and morning came, and this was the sixth day.

This was how the universe was completed. By the seventh day, God had finished His creation and needed to rest. He blessed the seventh day because it was His special day of rest.

Did you know?

The day of rest is called the Sabbath. Many people do not work on this day to worship God.

Eve's Temptation

Genesis 3:6 The woman saw how beautiful the tree was and how good its fruit would be to eat, and she thought how wonderful it would be to become wise.

Did you know?

In Hebrew, the name Adam means "mankind."

God planted a beautiful garden called Eden for Adam to live in. It was a wonderful garden filled with animals, plants, and flowers, including trees bearing delicious fruit for them to eat. God also planted two special trees – the tree of life and the tree of the knowledge of good and evil.

"You may eat the fruit from every tree in the garden, except the tree of the knowledge of good and evil," God told Adam. "For if you do, you will die."

Adam lived happily in the Garden of Eden until he realized that he was lonely. Seeing this, God waited until Adam was asleep and carefully took out one of his ribs. From this, He made a woman named Eve. She was the first woman God created, and she became Adam's wife.

Adam and Eve were very happy together in the Garden of Eden until one day when they were confronted by a cunning snake.

"Did God really tell you not to eat from the tree of the knowledge of good and evil?" asked the snake.

"Yes," said Eve. "If Adam or I even touch the fruit from the special tree, we will die."

"Oh, that isn't true," hissed the snake. "God only told you that because He knows that when you eat from that tree, you will become like Him. You will know what is good and what is evil."

The devious snake slithered through the grass and quickly wound its way up the tree of the knowledge of good and evil.

Looking up, Eve could see the fruit hanging from the tree, enticing her to eat it. Unable to resist, Eve picked the fruit and began to eat it. Then, as the snake wriggled away, Eve offered some to Adam.

Suddenly, everything in Eden seemed different. The fruit from the tree of the knowledge of good and evil had given Adam and Eve understanding. Realizing they were naked, they tied together fig leaves to cover their bodies.

"Where are you?" called God, as Adam tried to hide his nakedness behind a bush. "Why did you eat the fruit from the forbidden tree?"

"Eve gave me the fruit," replied Adam, bowing his head in shame.

"It was the snake's fault. He told me that if I ate the fruit, I would become as wise as you," said Eve.

Filled with anger, God punished Adam and Eve. "Through your disobedience, pain and suffering have come into the world," God told them. "From now on, your lives will be marked by hardship and suffering." With that, they were banished from the Garden of Eden forever.

Cain and Abel

Genesis 4:7 "If you had done the right thing, you would be smiling; but because you have done evil, sin is crouching at your door. It wants to rule you, but you must overcome it."

After they had disobeyed God, life became very hard for Adam and Eve. But they found happiness in their two sons, Cain and Abel.

Abel grew up to become a shepherd, tending his flocks in the hills and always watching over them in all weathers. Cain became a farmer. Every day, he would go out into the fields, digging the earth, ready to plant seeds.

One day, Cain chose some of his crops, a few vegetables, and some fruit to give as an offering to God. His offering was not the best of all he had grown, but Cain thought it was reasonable enough. After all, God had the whole world, so the quality of Cain's offering could not be that important, could it?

Abel was more thoughtful and believed that everything he had belonged to God, so he offered the Lord the finest sheep from his flock.

God was pleased with Abel's gift, but He rejected Cain's offering. Cain was furious and began to shout at his younger brother.

God told Cain, "If you had given freely to me like your brother, then you would have won my approval, too. Instead, you resented giving me even the smallest amount of food."

Unwilling to listen to God's words, Cain asked Abel to walk with him in the fields. But as soon as they were alone together, Cain killed his brother.

"Cain, where is your brother, Abel?" asked God.

"I have no idea," said Cain. "Am I my brother's keeper?"

But God had seen what Cain had done and said, in a voice filled with rage, "Why have you done this terrible thing? I can clearly see your brother's blood on your hands! For your terrible sins, you must leave this land to wander the earth aimlessly forever."

"But God, whoever meets me will know you have punished me and will want to kill me themselves."

God showed the extent of his mercy, telling Cain, "I will protect you. If anyone kills you, seven lives will be taken in revenge."

With that, God put a mark on Cain to warn people not to kill him, before sending him to the land of Nod to wander the earth forever.

Did you know?

Today, to go to the land of Nod means to go to sleep.

Noah's Ark

Genesis 7:1 The Lord said to Noah, "Go into the boat with your whole family; I have found that you are the only one in all the world who does what is right."

As the centuries passed, God became disappointed with the bad lives people had chosen to live. But there was one man who pleased Him. His name was Noah.

"I am very disappointed with the people I have created, so I have decided to punish them by flooding the world," God told him. "But because you have lived such a good life, I shall save you and your family."

God told Noah to build an ark that would be big enough for him and his wife, their three sons and their wives, and two of every kind of animal and bird. Just as Noah had finished building the ark, it began to rain, so Noah filled the ark with hundreds of creatures.

For many days, the rain fell. Rivers overflowed, and everything outside the ark perished. After a hundred and fifty days, the water level began to drop, and the ark came to rest on the tip of Mount Ararat.

Noah wanted to know if the earth was dry enough for everyone to leave the boat, so he released one of the ravens from the ark to see if it could find land. But the raven did not return. Noah then released a dove, but it returned with no news.

After another seven days, Noah released the dove again. This time it returned the same evening, carrying an olive branch in its beak. It had found dry land!

Did you know?

Noah's grandfather was Methuselah, the oldest person in the Bible. He died aged nine hundred and sixty nine in the year of the Flood.

The Rainbow Promise

Genesis 8:21 "Never again will I put the earth under a curse because of what people do; I know that from the time they are young their thoughts are evil," said the Lord.

When Noah, his family, and all the animals and birds were safely on dry land, God looked down upon them and made a promise.

"Now that you are back on land, you are free to find new homes for your families. The animals must be released so that they, too, can find new homes and the world can become full again," said God. "But I promise that no matter how wickedly people decide to live their lives, never again will I send a flood to destroy the earth. If it rains for a long time, and you fear that I have forgotten this promise, look up at the sky and I will show you a sign that I have not forgotten."

As Noah and his family looked up, a beautiful rainbow arched across the sky.

"The rainbow will always remind you of my promise to every creature that roams this land, for now and for all of time," God said to them.

In the years that followed, Noah, who lived to be a very old man, often looked up at the beautiful rainbows in the sky and remembered God's promise. He served God faithfully every day of his long and happy life.

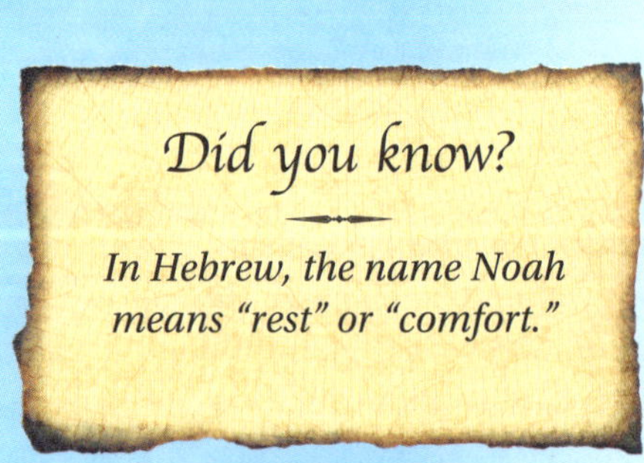

Did you know?

In Hebrew, the name Noah means "rest" or "comfort."

The Tower of Babel

Genesis 11:4 They said, "Now let's build a city with a tower that reaches the sky, so that we can make a name for ourselves and not be scattered all over the earth."

After the great flood, all of Noah's descendants spread over the earth in various directions. A group of people decided they would like to make a home for themselves in Babylonia. Shortly afterward, they began talking with each other to make plans for how they would build their houses.

As people learned to make bricks and how to build, they planned to make bigger and better buildings. One day, some of the people suggested they build not just houses but a huge, magnificent city. "We can even make the tallest tower in the world, and then we'll be the best!" they cheered.

God watched as people eagerly began working on the tower. He saw the walls getting higher and the people's ideas getting bigger. He knew that before long, they would all think they could do anything – and that nothing was impossible. These people were beginning to think they were gods among men!

So, before the tower was finished, God decided to punish them for their vanity by confusing their language. Where people all used to speak the same language, from that day on, they would all speak different languages.

There was chaos! The builders could not understand a word they were saying to each other, and the people could no longer make their great plans.

The great tower was left unfinished and became known as the Tower of Confusion, or the Tower of Babel.

God's Promise to Abraham

Genesis 12:2 "I will give you many descendants, and they will become a great nation. I will bless you and make your name famous, so that you will be a blessing," said the Lord.

Abraham and his wife, Sarah, lived in the city of Haran. Although they were wealthy and had many possessions, the couple could not have the one thing they truly wanted – a child of their own.

Abraham's nephew, Lot, was like a son to him. But the sight of Lot, who already had children of his own, only made Sarah unhappy.

One day, as Abraham reflected on how lucky he and his wife had been, he heard a voice. As if in a dream, the voice said, "Abraham, I am the Lord, your God. You must leave your people and your father's house and go to the land of Canaan."

Abraham was a good man and knew that he must obey the command of God. So, the next day, Abraham and Sarah journeyed south to Canaan. Abraham's nephew, Lot, and Lot's family went with them.

When they arrived, God spoke to Abraham. "For your faith, I will reward you with a son. Look around you; this is the country that I am going to give to your descendants," He said.

To show how grateful he was, Abraham and his family went to different parts of Canaan, building altars to worship God at each place they visited.

Abraham in Egypt

Genesis 12:16 Because of her, the king treated Abraham well and gave him flocks of sheep and goats, cattle, donkeys, slaves, and camels.

After Abraham and his family had been in Canaan for some time, there was a terrible famine, and this forced them to move farther south into Egypt to find food.

As they were about to cross the border into Egypt, Abraham said, "You are very beautiful, Sarah. If the Egyptians know that you are my wife, they will kill me because they will be jealous of me. You must pretend to be my sister; then they will treat me well."

When the king of Egypt heard how beautiful Abraham's "sister" was, he took her to live in his palace. Just as he had guessed, Abraham was treated well by the king and was given many gifts.

But God was angry with the king for taking Sarah away from Abraham and sent terrible diseases to punish him and all who lived in his palace.

When the king of Egypt discovered that Sarah was married to Abraham, he could not understand why Abraham had not told him the truth, and he was furious for the punishment he had received from God. The king had Abraham, Sarah, and their belongings thrown out of the palace and out of Egypt.

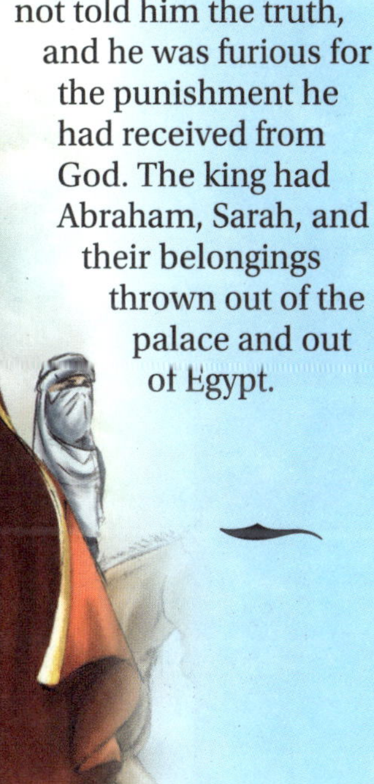

Lot's Choice

Genesis 13:8 Then Abraham said to Lot, "We are relatives, and your men and my men shouldn't be arguing. So let's separate.

After leaving Egypt, Abraham and his family journeyed back to the southern part of Canaan, settling in the place where Abraham had once built an altar to worship God.

Both Abraham and his nephew, Lot, were very wealthy men, and each owned many sheep, goats, and cattle. But this meant that they both needed plenty of land to keep and graze their animals. Soon, Abraham's herdsmen and Lot's herdsmen began to argue over the best place to keep their animals. Each day, the men's arguments grew louder and fiercer, with fists being raised and stones being thrown.

Abraham was saddened to see all the herdsmen, who had once been friends, now shouting and threatening each other over the best pasture when land was so plentiful.

"Why don't we settle in different places?" Abraham suggested to his nephew. "Then our animals can spread out and graze wherever they want."

A kind and generous man, Abraham told Lot that he could have first choice of where he wanted to live.

So Lot made his way with his family, the herdsmen, sheep, goats, and cattle to the Jordan Valley, while Abraham stayed in Canaan.

Hagar and Ishmael

Genesis 16:11 The angel of the Lord said to her, "You are going to have a baby. You shall bear a son, who you will name Ishmael."

Despite being nearly eighty years old, there was never a day that passed when Abraham's wife, Sarah, did not wish for a son of her own. She remembered the promise God had made to Abraham, but as the years passed, Sarah grew more troubled.

One day, Sarah looked at her beautiful Egyptian slave, Hagar, and thought that perhaps she could give Abraham a son instead.

At first, Abraham did not like the idea, but Sarah persisted. "But Hagar is my servant," Sarah told him, "She is young and beautiful and can give us the child we so desperately want."

And so, within a short time, Hagar became pregnant. Sarah's plan had worked, and she was delighted.

But soon after, Sarah became jealous of Hagar. She treated her so badly that Hagar ran away into the desert. As the hot sun burned her skin and she became desperately thirsty, Hagar fell to her knees in the sand. As she looked up to the sky, she saw an angel of the Lord.

"I know it is hard, but you must go back to your mistress," said the angel. "Soon you will give birth to a son, who shall be named Ishmael."

Obeying the angel, Hagar went back to Abraham and Sarah, then gave birth to a boy, just as the angel had told her she would.

Abraham looked down fondly as he held the baby in his arms. He did not realize that this was not the child that God had promised to him and Sarah.

Sodom and Gomorrah

Genesis 19:15 At dawn, the angels tried to make Lot hurry. "Quick!" they said. "Take your wife and your two daughters and get out, so that you will not lose your lives when the city is destroyed."

After leaving Canaan, Abraham's nephew, Lot, settled with his wife and children near the cities of Sodom and Gomorrah.

But as the years passed, the people in these cities began to ignore God's teachings and lived sinful lives.

Angry at the way his people had turned their backs on him, God decided to destroy Sodom and all the other cities around it. Only Lot and his family, who had lived honest lives and had faithfully served the Lord, would be saved.

God sent two angels to Sodom to warn Lot about the terrible disaster that was about to befall his home.

The two angels took Lot, his wife, and their two daughters by the hand, then pulled them out of their house, saying, "You must leave here now and go to the mountains, where you will be safe. Do not look behind you. The Lord has heard terrible things about the people of Sodom, and He is going to destroy the city and its people!"

But as they fled the city, Lot's wife could not resist looking back one last time - and she was turned into a pillar of salt.

The Birth of Isaac

Genesis 21:8 The child grew, and on the day that he was weaned, Abraham gave a great feast.

When he was ninety-nine years old, God visited Abraham and told him that his wife, Sarah, would soon give him a son. Abraham was very surprised to hear this and wondered if a man could have a child when he was almost a hundred years old!

"Can Sarah really give birth to a child even though she is ninety years old?" Abraham asked God. "Why not just let Ishmael, my son by Hagar, be my heir?"

"No, your wife Sarah will bear you a son, and you will name him Isaac," said the Lord, who had other plans for Ishmael.

When Sarah learned that she was to bear Abraham a son, she was shocked and found it very hard to believe that she would become pregnant at such an old age. But the Lord kept his promise, and exactly nine months later, when Abraham was a hundred years old, Sarah gave birth to a son. Abraham named the boy Isaac, as God had told him to do.

"After so many years of longing for a child of my own, God has brought me joy and laughter," said Sarah. "Everyone who hears about the birth of Isaac will be overjoyed and wish us great happiness."

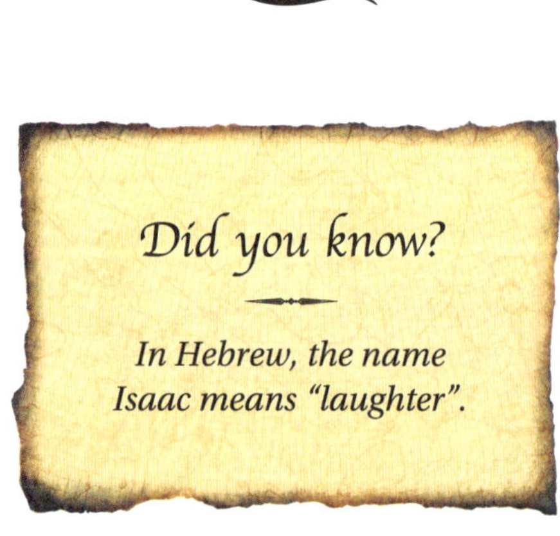

Abraham's Test

Genesis 22:15 "I promise that I will give you as many descendants as there are stars in the sky or grains of sand along the seashore. Your descendants will conquer their enemies."

Isaac grew up to be a wonderful son to Abraham and Sarah. God saw that they were very happy and decided to test Abraham's faith.

One day, God told Abraham, "Take your son, Isaac, to the land of Moriah. When you get there, you must offer him as a sacrifice to me."

Sadness and rage filled Abraham's heart. How could the Lord ask him to kill the son he loved so much? But Abraham knew he had to do as God commanded. Abraham set off the next morning with Isaac and two servants.

After journeying for three days, Abraham saw Moriah in the distance.

"Stay here," he commanded the servants, "while Isaac and I go and pray."

Abraham made an altar of bricks and tied Isaac on it. With tears in his eyes, he raised his knife to kill the son he loved so dearly.

Suddenly, the angel of the Lord called out to him, "Do not hurt the boy! The Lord sees that you worship and obey him, since you were prepared to offer your son to him despite your sadness."

For his obedience, God showered Abraham with blessings and told him that he would have as many descendants as there were glittering stars in the sky.

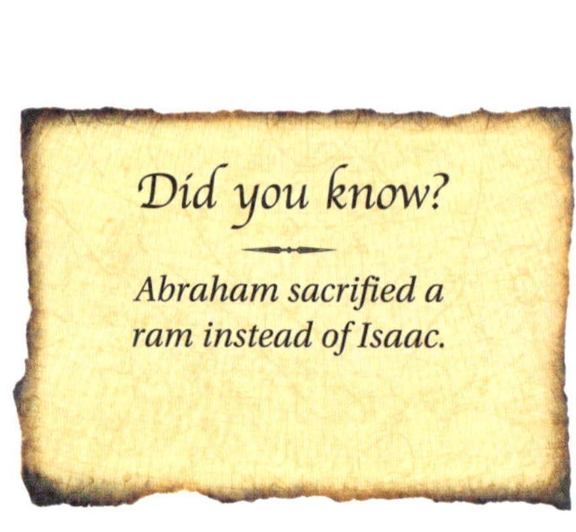

Isaac and Rebekah

Genesis 24:3 "I want you to make a vow in the name of the Lord, the God of Heaven and earth, that you will not choose a wife for my son from the people here in Canaan," said Abraham.

As the years passed, Isaac grew up to be strong and kind, and Abraham was very proud of him. When Sarah died, Abraham knew that it would soon be his time, too.

"It is important for my son, Isaac, to marry and have a family of his own," he told his oldest servant. "When I am no longer here, you must find him a wife – not from here in Canaan, but from Haran, the country where I was born. God promised that he would give this land to my descendants, so he will send an angel to go with you."

The servant took ten of his master's camels and went to Abraham's old home, along with some other servants. At Haran, as their camels rested near a well, the servant prayed to God.

"Here I am at the well where the young women of the city will come soon to get water. When I say to a woman, 'Lower your jar and let me have a drink,' and she replies, 'Drink, and I will fetch water for your camels,' let her be the one you have chosen for Isaac."

Before he had even finished praying, a girl named Rebekah arrived at the well, carrying a jar of water on her shoulder.

"Drink," said Rebekah, when the servant asked for some of her water. "And I will fetch more water for your camels."

After watching Rebekah for a while, the servant took a gold ring and two gold bracelets from his bag and put them on the girl. "Whose daughter are you – and is there enough room for us to stay in your father's house tonight?" he asked.

"My father is Bethuel, son of Nahor and Milcah," the girl answered, "and yes, we have plenty of room for you to stay."

The servant fell to his knees and said, "Praise the Lord, who has kept his promise to my master Abraham. Thank you for guiding me straight to the house of my master's relatives."

Rebekah smiled fondly, for she had heard many wonderful stories about her father's uncle Abraham, who had left his home to follow the command of God.

Later, when the servant was sharing a meal with Rebekah's family, he told them about Abraham's son, Isaac, and how he had been sent to find a wife for him.

Bethuel and Rebekah's brother Laban understood that the Lord had chosen Rebekah to be Isaac's wife.

"You must take my daughter and go, for the Lord has spoken," said Bethuel. And so Rebekah returned with the servants to become Isaac's wife.

Jacob and Esau

Genesis 27:24 And he said, "Are you really my son Esau?" And he said, "I am."

After many years, Rebekah gave birth to twin boys named Jacob and Esau. God said that one day, Jacob would be the head of the family, even though Esau was in fact the elder of the two.

Isaac preferred his oldest son, Esau, who was a skilled hunter, but Rebekah preferred Jacob, who was quiet and thoughtful.

When Isaac was very old and going blind, he told Esau to go hunting for some meat. "When you have made me a tasty stew with the meat, I will give you my final blessing before I die," he said weakly.

Rebekah was determined that Jacob would receive the blessing to rule the family instead of Esau. So, when Esau had left the house, she told Jacob to fetch two goats from the field, which she used to make a stew. Rebekah then told Jacob to dress in some of Esau's clothes, so that Isaac would not recognize him, and to put the goatskins on his arms to make them like Esau's hairy arms.

"Which son are you?" asked Isaac, when Jacob gave him the stew.

"I am Esau," said Jacob, leaning over to kiss his father's face.

Isaac could smell Esau's clothes on Jacob and feel his hairy arms, so he gave the younger son his blessing. Jacob was now to be the head of the family after Isaac's death.

Jacob's Ladder

Genesis 28:20-21 Then Jacob made a vow to the Lord. "If you are with me and protect me on the journey I am making and give me food and clothing, and if I return safely to my father's home, then you will be my God."

When Esau learned that Jacob had tricked his father, he was extremely angry. Rebekah then sent Jacob away to live with her brother, Laban, in a city called Haran.

On his way to Haran, Jacob stopped to rest. He fell asleep and dreamed he saw a stairway reaching from the earth to Heaven, with angels floating up and down on it. At the very top of the stairway there was a brilliant light, and a voice said, "I am the Lord, the God of Abraham and Isaac. I will give you and all of your descendants all this land that you are resting on and the land all around it. Through you and your many descendants, I will bless all the nations. Wherever you go, I will protect you and bring you back to this land. I will never leave you until I have done all that I have promised you."

"The Lord is here - and he is with me!" thought Jacob, when he woke the next morning.

Taking the stone he had used to rest his head, Jacob set it up as a memorial to God. Although he felt a little afraid, Jacob was also happy. "I have found the house of God!" he said. "This must be the gate that opens into Heaven."

Jacob Is Tricked

Genesis 29:25 He went to Laban and said, "Why did you do this to me? I worked for you in order to marry Rachel. Why have you tricked me?"

When Jacob arrived in Haran, he did not know how to find his relatives, so he asked some shepherds who were sitting beside a well.

"We are from Haran, and we know your uncle, Laban," said the shepherds, as a shepherd girl came to the well with her flock. The shepherds told Jacob that the girl's name was Rachel and that she was one of the two daughters of Laban.

As soon as he saw her, Jacob fell in love with Rachel. "Your father is my uncle," Jacob told her. "Please tell him that the son of Rebekah has come to see him."

On hearing the news of his arrival, Laban hurried to meet Jacob and listened to everything Jacob told him, including how he had tricked his own brother. Shortly after, Jacob began working for his uncle.

One day, Laban said, "It is not right for a nephew of mine to work without pay. How much should I pay you, Jacob?"

All Jacob could think about was Rachel. "I will work for you for seven years without pay, if I can then marry Rachel," he said.

After seven years of hard work, the day of the wedding arrived. After the ceremony, Jacob and his wife went home. But when his bride removed her veil, Jacob realized that Laban had tricked him into marrying the wrong sister! Just as Jacob had once pretended to be his older brother, so Leah had pretended to be her younger sister.

When Jacob complained to Laban, Laban suggested that Jacob work a further seven years for him, after which time he would be given Rachel as his wife as well.

Jacob Wrestles God

Genesis 32:25 When the man saw that he was not winning the struggle, he struck Jacob on the hip, and it was thrown out of joint.

After marrying Leah's sister, Rachel, Jacob decided to return to Canaan with his family. Jacob was afraid that Esau would kill them all, so he sent messengers ahead to make peace with his brother. But the messengers returned with the news that Esau was on his way with four hundred men!

Jacob prayed to God for help. Suddenly, a man appeared in the dark and started to wrestle with Jacob. They wrestled all night.

"Let me go now," said the man, as daybreak came.

But Jacob would not let go, even when the stranger injured his hip. "Not unless you bless me!" he said, knowing that this was no ordinary man.

"Tell me your name!" demanded the man.

"Jacob."

"No," said the stranger. "From this day, you will be named Israel because you have struggled with God and with men, and you have won."

And then the man blessed Jacob and disappeared.

Jacob trembled. "I have seen God face to face, and yet I am still alive!" he said.

He named the place he wrestled with the stranger "Peniel," which means "the face of God" in Hebrew.

In the distance, Jacob saw Esau coming toward him. But instead of causing any trouble, Esau ran to Jacob and hugged him.

Joseph's Special Coat

Genesis 37:3 Jacob loved Joseph more than all his other sons because he had been born to him when he was old.

Jacob had twelve sons, including Rachel's two boys, Joseph and Benjamin. When Rachel died, Joseph became the son he loved best.

Jacob spoiled Joseph and gave him a special coat which was all the hues of the rainbow. Joseph's brothers felt that this coat should have been given to the firstborn son. This made the other brothers jealous.

The brothers hated Joseph even more when he told them about his dreams, where he had seen them and his father all bowing down to him.

"Huh! So you think you are going to be a king and rule over us, do you?" they sneered. Even Jacob was angry when he heard about the dreams.

When Joseph went out to check his flocks one day, his brothers kidnapped him and sold him to some merchants who were passing by.

After staining Joseph's special coat with animal blood, the brothers showed it to Jacob. "Some wild animals attacked Joseph and ripped him to pieces in the field," they said.

Poor Jacob was inconsolable. "Now I will live in sorrow until the day I die," he sobbed.

Joseph in Egypt

Genesis 39:6 Potiphar handed over everything he had to the care of Joseph and did not concern himself with anything, except the food he ate.

Joseph was sold as a slave to Potiphar, an officer of the king of Egypt. With God watching over him, Joseph worked hard and was successful in everything he did, which soon attracted his master's attention.

Realizing that his new slave was different to all his other servants, Potiphar put Joseph in charge of his household and all his business.

While Potiphar spent all his time eating, drinking, and having a good time, Joseph took care of everything.

Joseph was a handsome man, and Potiphar's wife fell in love with him. But Joseph was loyal to Potiphar, who had treated him well. So, when his master's wife made advances toward him, Joseph rejected her.

To be turned away by a servant was a great insult, so Potiphar's wife lied and told the other servants that Joseph had tried to attack her. "When I screamed, he ran away like a coward, leaving his coat behind!" she said.

Even Potiphar believed his wife's lies and had Joseph arrested and thrown in prison. But even there, God was with Joseph and helped him every day.

Did you know?

The brothers' first plan was to kill Joseph. But the oldest brother, Rueben, pursuaded the others not to do this. He wanted to save Joseph.

The King's Dream

Genesis 41:56 The famine grew worse and spread over the whole country, so Joseph opened all the storehouses and sold grain to the Egyptians.

Joseph soon became known inside the prison for being able to explain what other people's dreams meant.

One day, a prisoner who had been the chief cupbearer to the king's court told Joseph about a dream that he had been having every night.

With God's help, Joseph told the man, "Your dream means that in three days time, you will return to your job as a cupbearer." And he did!

Two years later, the king of Egypt had a strange dream, and the cupbearer remembered Joseph. The king told Joseph that in his dream, he was standing by the Nile River, when seven fat cows came out of the water. Then seven thin cows followed, and the thin cows ate up all the fat cows!

"God has told you what he is going to do," said Joseph. "There will be seven years of good harvests, followed by seven years of famine. If you behave wisely, you can store plenty of food in the good years, so that your people won't starve in the bad ones."

The king thought Joseph was very wise, so he made him the governor of Egypt. For the next seven years, Joseph, who was given many riches, journeyed throughout the land, organizing all the food supplies, so that no one would starve during the famine.

The Great Famine

Genesis 42:21 "Yes, now we are suffering the consequences of what we did to our brother; we saw the great trouble he was in when he begged for help, but we would not listen. That is why we are in this trouble now."

Just as Joseph had predicted, after the seven years of abundance came a great and devastating famine.

In Canaan, when Jacob heard that there was plenty of grain in Egypt, he told all his sons, except Benjamin, the youngest, to go there and buy some.

When the ten brothers stood before the governor of Egypt to ask for grain, they had no idea who he was. But Joseph recognized them and decided to see if they were as cruel as they had once been. "You are spies!" he said.

"No. We are just a family of brothers," they told him. "There used to be twelve of us, but the youngest brother has stayed with our father, and the other brother died many years ago."

Joseph then demanded they prove they were telling the truth. Keeping one brother, Simeon, as a hostage, he told the others to go home and return with Benjamin. But first, he made sure that their bags were filled with grain - and secretly hid the money they had paid for the grain in their sacks.

When the brothers told their father that they must return to Egypt with Benjamin, he was unhappy. But Jacob knew he had no choice.

The Family Reunion

Genesis 45:28 "My son Joseph is still alive!" he said. "This is all I could ask for! I must go and see him before I die."

When Joseph saw Benjamin, he could hardly stop himself from showing his great happiness. "Let a banquet be served!" he said.

Joseph's brothers didn't understand why such an important man would provide a banquet for them. But they ate all the same.

Next morning, when their sacks had been filled with grain, Joseph told his servants to return the brothers' money and to hide his own silver cup in Benjamin's sack.

Still unaware that the governor of Egypt was their own brother, the men set off for Canaan. But they had only gone

a short way when one of Joseph's servants caught up with them. "Why have you treated my master like this?" he asked. "You have repaid his kindness by stealing his precious silver cup!"

"We would never do such a terrible thing!" said the brothers.

Of course, just as Joseph had planned, the servant soon found the cup hidden in Benjamin's sack!

Returning to the city, the brothers fell at Joseph's feet and humbly begged his forgiveness.

"We beg you to take pity on us!" said Judah, "To prove our innocence, we offer ourselves to be your servants."

"No," replied Joseph. "You may all go free, except the one whose sack contained my cup. He shall be my slave!"

But the brothers could not bear to return home with the news that their father had had another son taken from him.

"Please don't take Benjamin," said Judah. "Our father has already lost one beloved son. If we don't bring Benjamin back with us, my father will die of grief. Let me be your slave in his place."

When Joseph heard this, he knew his brothers were truly sorry for their past cruelty. Sending his servants away, he said, "Don't you know me? I am Joseph, your brother."

The brothers were afraid, but Joseph told them not to be. "God sent me to Egypt to save many lives, including yours," he said. "Go home and bring the rest of the family here, to live near me."

So Jacob and Joseph's brothers, and their wives, children, and servants left Canaan and came to Egypt.

Jacob wept with joy when he saw that the son he had believed to be dead was now a great man, the governor of all Egypt!

Did you know?

Jacob made Joseph promise that when he died, he would bury him in the land of Canaan, where God had promised to make Jacob's descendants into a great nation.

Baby Moses

Exodus 2:9 The princess told the woman, "Take this baby and nurse him for me, and I will pay you."

Jacob's descendants, the Israelites, grew to be a powerful nation – and the Egyptians were afraid of them. When a new king came to the throne, he decided to do something about these people, before it was too late.

The cruel king made the Israelites his slaves. Slave drivers forced them to make heavy bricks out of mud and to drag huge stones for the building of new cities.

The Israelites worked hard from dawn till dusk. If they dared to slacken their pace, a slave driver or two would use his powerful whip on them!

But no matter how hard they were worked, still the Israelites grew in numbers. So the king ordered his soldiers to hurl every baby boy into the Nile River.

During this terrible time, an Israelite woman gave birth to a boy. After three months, she knew she couldn't hide the child inside her house much longer without someone hearing his cries. So, with no other choice, she took a basket of reeds and covered it with tar, to make it watertight. Then she put her tiny baby inside and set him afloat among the tall reeds and bulrushes by the riverbank.

As the baby's sister, Miriam, watched the basket floating on the water, the king's daughter waded into the water to bathe. Suddenly, she saw something floating in the distance. She told her maids to fetch the strange object and bring it to her.

Did you know?

At first, the king of Egypt asked the Israelite midwives to kill every baby boy at birth, but they refused.

When the princess opened the basket and saw a crying child inside, her heart melted. She had never seen such a beautiful baby!

"This must be one of the Israelite babies," she said, holding the child close to her breast. "I will bring up this baby as my own and name him Moses."

When Miriam, who had been hiding, heard what the princess had said, she walked toward her and in a timid voice said, "Princess, would you like me to fetch an Israelite woman to look after the baby?"

"Yes, yes, that would be a wonderful idea," said the princess.

So the baby's own mother took care of him in her own home until he was old enough to go to the palace, to live as the princess's own son.

Prince of Egypt

Exodus 2:15-16 When the king heard about what had happened, he tried to have Moses killed, but Moses fled and went to live in the land of Midian.

Moses grew up as a royal prince of Egypt and was given everything he could ever want. But despite his wealthy, privileged life, Moses never forgot where he came from – or that he was an Israelite. It made him sad to see how cruelly his people were treated.

One day, as Moses was out walking, he saw a slave driver mercilessly beating an Israelite slave.

"Stop! Stop!" called Moses, but the slave driver ignored his cries and then continued his brutal ill-treatment of the poor slave.

Moses was filled with rage, and before he knew what he was doing, he struck down the Egyptian and killed him! Feeling guilty, Moses tried to hide the body, but word soon spread about what he had done.

When the king heard that Moses had taken the side of an Israelite against an Egyptian, he ordered his arrest. But Moses ran away, leaving his life as an Egyptian prince far behind.

As he wandered into the hot desert, Moses knew that he might never see his family, or the Israelite people, ever again.

Moses and the Burning Bush

Exodus 3:2 There, the angel of the Lord appeared to him as a flame from the middle of a bush. Moses looked, and although the bush was on fire, it was not burning up.

Moses escaped to Midian and married Zipporah, the daughter of Jethro, the priest of Midian.

One day, as Moses led Jethro's flocks across the desert, he came to Sinai, the holy mountain – and the voice of the Lord came to him from a burning bush.

Although the bush seemed to be on fire, it was not burning away as it should have been.

"Moses!" said God. "I am the God of your ancestors. I have seen how cruelly my people are being treated in Egypt, and I am sending you to rescue them. I have chosen you to lead them to the land I have promised to my people."

"But what do I say if the Israelites ask who has sent me?" asked Moses.

God said, "I am who I am. You must say, 'The one who is called I AM has sent me to you.'"

"But what if they don't believe me?" said Moses. God told Moses to throw his staff on the ground – and it turned into a snake. Then, as Moses grabbed it by the tail, it became a staff of wood once again.

God gave Moses other miracles to perform, and said, "I am sending your brother, Aaron, to you. He is a good speaker, and you can pass on my message through him to all the people."

The Terrible Plagues

Exodus 8:5 The Lord said to Moses, "Tell Aaron to hold out his stick over the rivers, the canals, and the pools, and make frogs come up and cover the land of Egypt."

Moses told Pharaoh that unless he allowed the Israelites to go free, God would punish him. To show the powers that God had given to him, Moses told Aaron to throw down his staff, which changed into a snake.

Pharaoh ordered his magicians to perform a similar trick with their staffs, and they did turn them into snakes, although Aaron's swallowed all theirs up.

God was very angry that Pharaoh would not free the Israelites, and He told Moses to summon terrible plagues.

First, the water in the Nile River turned blood red and all the fish died.

Then, a plague of frogs descended on the land of Egypt. But still Pharaoh would not change his mind.

Then came swarms of insects and gnats, followed by a plague of flies.

As with the other plagues, only the Israelites were left alone.

More plagues followed. The cattle and sheep began to die; every Egyptian had painful boils; and huge hailstones fell from the sky. But Pharaoh still refused God's demands.

So God sent a swarm of locusts, which ate all the crops, followed by a terrible darkness that lasted three days.

Finally, God told Moses to prepare for the worst plague of all. The firstborn son in every Egyptian household would die!

Did you know?

Moses' name is made up of two words that together mean "to come out of the water."

The Passover

Exodus 12:3 That night, the king, his officials, and all the other Egyptians were awakened. There was loud crying throughout Egypt because there was not one home in which there was not a dead son.

God told Moses that when He sent the final plague, the Israelites would leave Egypt that same night. Then He gave Moses instructions for the Israelites, telling them how they must protect their firstborn sons.

Every Israelite family had to kill a young male lamb or goat and put some of the blood around the door of their house. Then they had to roast the lamb and eat it with herbs and flat loaves of bread made without yeast.

"When God comes to bring judgement and sees the sign of blood above your doors, He will pass over your houses, and your children will be safe," Moses told the Israelites.

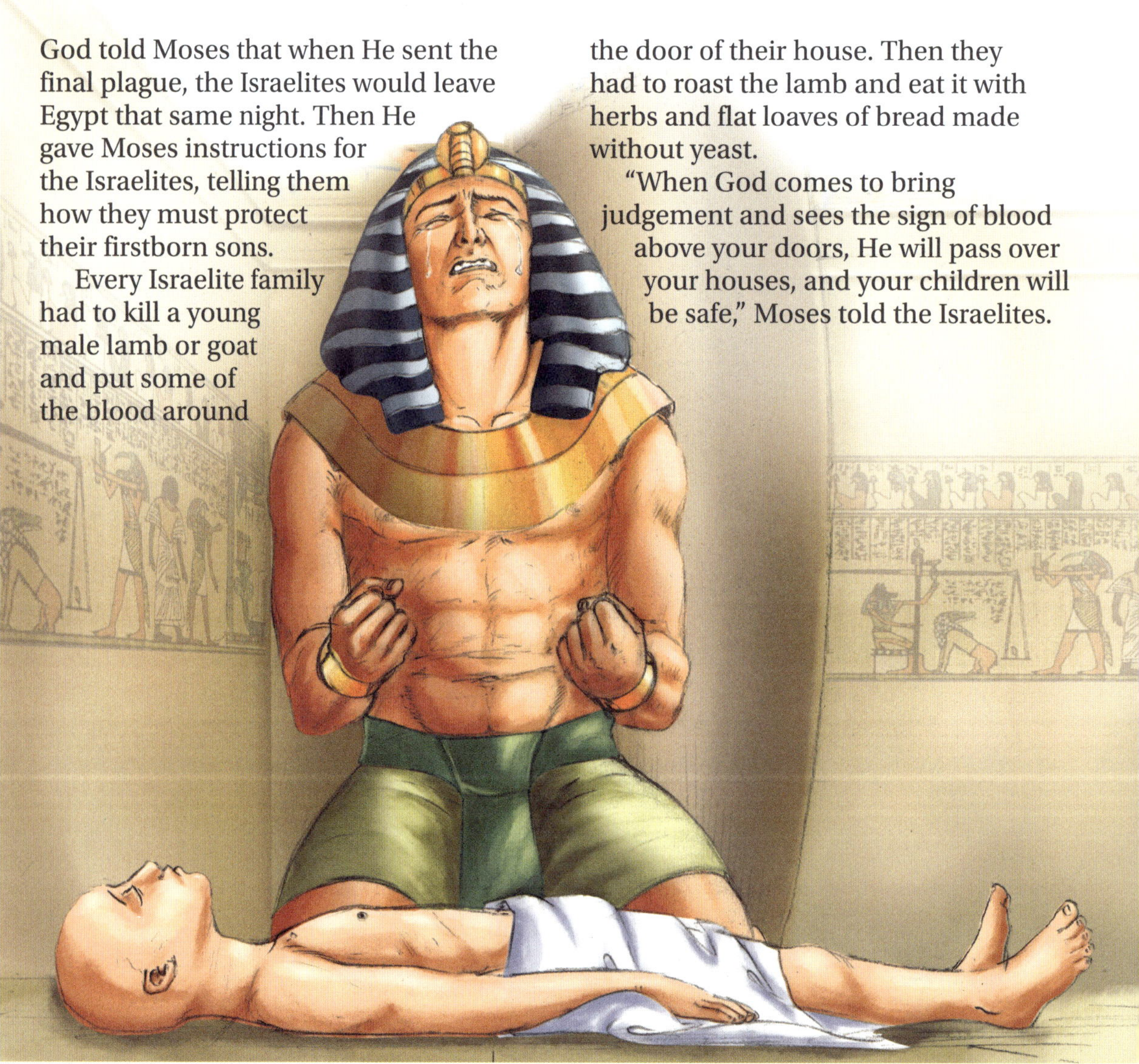

At midnight, God passed over every house where He saw the mark of blood, but He struck dead every firstborn Egyptian baby boy, from the king's own son and heir, down to the sons of prisoners in the dungeon.

When Pharaoh, the king of Egypt, discovered the dead body of his own firstborn, he knew that he had brought this destruction on his country because of his cruelty.

Escape from Egypt

Exodus 12:33 The Egyptians urged the people to hurry and leave the country; they said, "We will all be dead if you don't leave."

Now that the Egyptians had all lost their firstborn sons, they couldn't wait for the Israelites to leave Egypt. Even Pharaoh begged Moses and Aaron to take their people far away from his land.

Many of the Egyptians respected Moses and understood why God had struck them with the most terrifying plagues. Pharaoh had treated the Israelites badly, forcing them into slavery and giving very little in return.

Did you know?

About 600,000 men, not counting women and children, left Egypt after God had sent the plagues.

As many thousands of Israelites marched out of Egypt, never to return, some of the Egyptians gave them gold and silver, cattle and sheep, and other precious gifts.

After living in Egypt for four hundred and thirty years, the Israelites were free! Never again would they be treated as slaves. Never again would they have to bear the indignity of cruel whippings and beatings.

Families wept tears of happiness as they helped each other along the dusty roads, getting closer and closer to their beloved home with each step they took.

Walking ahead, Moses knew he would lead his people safely home. As he looked up at the night sky, Moses thanked God for all He had done – and for keeping His promise as He spoke from the burning bush on Mount Sinai, "I am who I am."

The Parting of the Red Sea

Exodus 14:13 Moses answered, "Don't be afraid! Stand your ground, and you will see what the Lord will do to save you today; you will never see these Egyptians again."

Almost as soon as Pharaoh had agreed to the Israelites leaving Egypt, he changed his mind. He wanted his slaves brought back, so they could continue building his cities.

So, led by Pharaoh himself, the bravest soldiers and all his chariots set off to recapture the Israelites.

Moses and his people were camped near the Red Sea. When they saw Pharaoh's army heading toward them, the Israelites were terrified. With the Egyptians on one side and water on the other, they were trapped!

"God will save you from the Egyptians," said Moses.

Then God spoke to Moses, telling him to stretch his hand out across the water.

"The Israelites will walk over on dry land, but the Egyptians will follow them to their deaths," said God.

Moses did as God said and stretched his arm out across the water. A fierce wind blew, and the Red Sea parted and formed two huge walls.

The Israelites walked safely between the two walls of water, raised by the angry wind. When the Egyptians saw this, they tried to follow, but Moses raised his hand once again - and this time, the walls of water collapsed! As every Egyptian disappeared under the water, the Israelites thanked God for saving them.

Manna from Heaven

Exodus 16:9 Moses said to Aaron, "Tell the whole community to come and stand before the Lord because He has heard their complaints."

At first, as they crossed the desert, the Israelites sang and danced and clapped their hands.

"We are free!" they laughed, sinking down on their knees to thank the Lord.

But as the sun beat down and sand from the desert filled their mouths and nostrils, the people quickly forgot all they had suffered at the hands of Pharaoh and his slave drivers.

They complained to Moses that the water in the stream was bitter and that they wanted food like they had tasted in Egypt.

"My people seem to have forgotten all the bad things that happened to them in Egypt," Moses told God. "Instead, all they can remember is the food they ate! What can I do to stop their constant complaints, dear Lord?"

God gave Moses a message to pass on to his people, "Tonight you will eat meat, and tomorrow I will rain down bread from Heaven."

Later that day, God sent them a flock of quails to eat. The next day, the sky rained manna, a type of special bread that tasted delicious, like biscuits made with honey.

Moses told the people, "God has asked that we fill a pot with manna and keep it forever, as a reminder that He will always provide for you, as He has today."

The people did this, so God sent manna to the Israelites every day for the forty years until they reached the land of Canaan, where they settled.

The Ten Commandments

Exodus 20:7 "Do not use my name for evil purposes, for I, the Lord your God, will punish anyone who misuses my name."

The Israelites made their way through the desert and reached Mount Sinai, the holy mountain of God – where He had appeared to Moses in the burning bush.

God came down to the mountain, and there was a light like a burning fire on top of the mountain. Cloud covered the mountain for six days. Leaving his people behind, Moses walked to the top of the mountain.

He entered the presence of God. God spoke to Moses, giving him Ten Commandments, or rules, by which God expected all people to live if they loved Him:

I am your God, who brought you out of Egypt. You must have no other gods but me.

You must not make any idols or bow down to them or worship them. You must worship me alone.

You must not misuse the name of the Lord your God.

Keep the Sabbath day holy. You can work for six days, but on the seventh, you must rest.

Respect your father and mother.

You must not commit murder.

You must not commit adultery.

You must not steal.

You must not tell lies.

Do not be jealous of anything belonging to other people.

Moses stayed on the mountain for forty days and nights, listening to God's words. Then, carrying the Ten Commandments on two slabs of stone, he came back down the mountain.

Did you know?

The Ten Commandments are the rules Jewish people follow about how to live. Many countries base their laws on these rules.

The Golden Calf

Exodus 32:14 So the Lord changed His mind and did not bring on His people the disaster He had threatened.

The Israelites trembled as the ground shook beneath them and thunder roared above their heads. But as silence fell and the sun shone down, they quickly forgot their fears. "Moses has been talking to God on Mount Sinai for too long!" they said.

Seeing their impatience, Aaron tried to calm them.

"You are Moses' brother. You can lead us and make us a good god to follow," said the people.

After some thought, Aaron agreed to make a new idol for them to worship.

He told the men to take their wives' earrings and bring them to him, so that he could melt them and cast a golden statue in the fire. When he had enough gold, he cast the statue into the shape of a calf. He then built an altar before it so that the people could worship their new god.

The crowd danced around the image singing, "This is our god who led us out of Egypt!"

When Moses came down from the mountain, he heard the people making a great noise. At first, he thought that they were at war, but then he realized that they were singing and dancing.

When God heard this, He told Moses that He was going to destroy the Israelites for glorifying the calf. But Moses pleaded with the Lord to forgive his people, and God spared them.

The people turned to see Moses carrying the slabs of stone on which God had written the Ten Commandments, and they saw that he was very angry. Raising up the slabs, he hurled them onto the rocks, where they shattered into pieces. The people knew that they had disobeyed God and felt ashamed.

Did you know?

Moses was on Mount Sinai for forty days and forty nights.

Moses Returns

Exodus 34:1 The Lord said to Moses, "Cut two stone tablets like the first ones, and I will write on them the words that were on the first tablets, which you broke."

In anger, Moses had broken the stone slabs bearing the Ten Commandments. Now he looked at Aaron, who had made a golden calf for the Israelites to worship.

Aaron made feeble excuses for what he had done, but Moses didn't believe him. So Moses used a large stone to grind the calf into powder, mixed it with water, and then made the people drink it!

God, who had seen everything, was willing to give the Israelites yet another chance to show their love for Him. He told Moses to come up the mountain one more time and to bring two new slabs of stone upon which God would write His commandments again.

When Moses reached the top of Mount Sinai, God made an agreement with him. "I will prepare a way to the land I have promised you," He said, "and I will help you to defeat all your enemies. But my people must never worship false idols and gods. I am the one, true God, so obey my commandments."

When the Israelites saw Moses holding the Ten Commandments again, they looked ashamed because they knew he had been standing in the presence of God.

The Journey Begins

Exodus 33:3 "You are going to a rich and fertile land. But I will not go with you myself, since you are a stubborn people, and I might destroy you on the way."

One day, God gave a message to Moses. He told him that it was time for him and the people he had brought out of Egypt to leave Mount Sinai.

"You must go to the land that I promised to give to Abraham, Isaac, and Jacob, and to all their descendants," said the Lord. "I will send an angel to watch over you, and I will drive your enemies away. But I will not go with you because you are a stubborn people, and I might very well become angry with you and destroy you on the way."

Moses gathered the crowd and repeated God's message to them, adding that God wanted them all to take off all their necklaces, bracelets, and earrings until he had decided what to do with them.

When the Israelites heard this, they began to mourn. "God is disappointed with us," they said, removing their fine trinkets.

And even after they had left Mount Sinai, the people of Israel no longer wore golden ornaments.

Moses' Mistake

Numbers 20:4 "Why have you brought us out into this wilderness? Just so that we can die here with our animals?"

Moving from place to place, the Israelites lived in the desert for many years. But the people were always complaining: There was never enough food, or there was never enough water – or it was far too hot!

One day, the Israelites were complaining about having no water again.

"Take the stick that is in front of the Covenant Box and then assemble the whole community," God told Moses and Aaron. "Then in front of the people, speak to the rock over there – and water will pour out of it."

But instead of doing as God had told him, Moses lost his temper with the ungrateful people to whom God had given so much. Picking up the stick, he banged it twice against the rock. "There," he shouted. "Will this stop you all complaining?"

Just as God had said, water flowed from the rock and into the sand, as it had done once before.

But God was disappointed with Moses, who had not fully obeyed His command.

"You did not show respect for my word before all the people, so I will not allow you to lead them into the Promised Land," He told Moses.

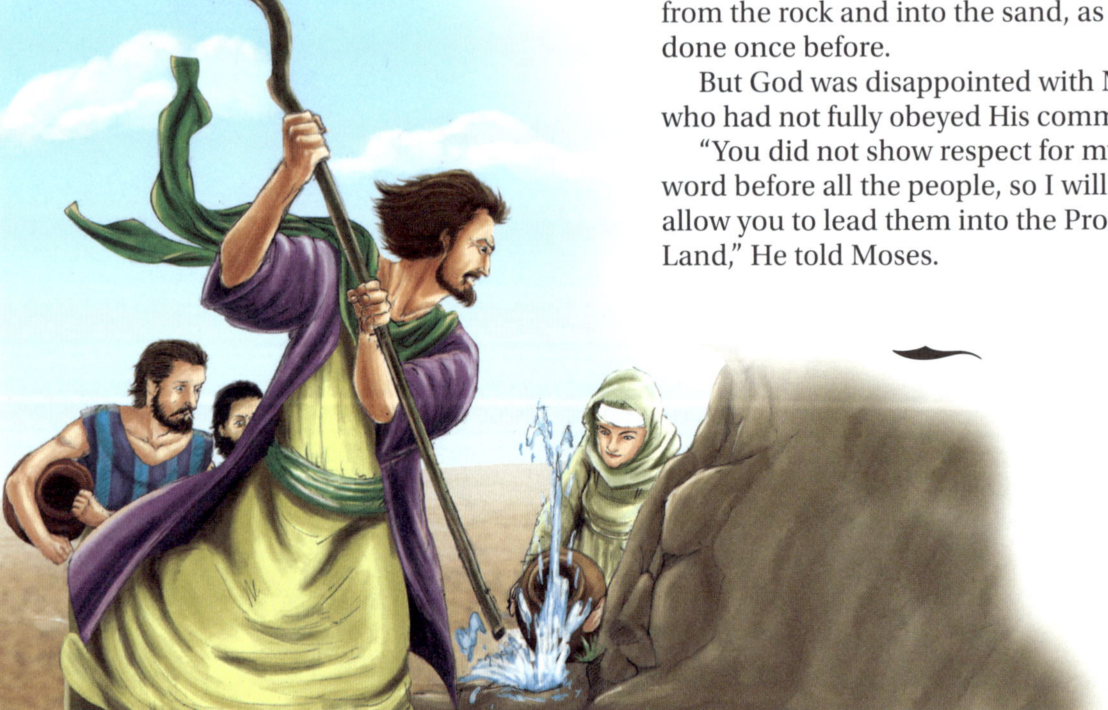

God and Balaam

Numbers 23:12 Balaam answered, "I can only say what the Lord tells me to say."

Balak, the king of Moab, wanted a prophet named Balaam to put a curse on the Israelites, who were entering Balak's lands. But God told Balaam not to do this, as the Israelites had His blessing.

"If Balak's men come to ask you to go with them, get ready to go," God told Balaam, "but do only what I tell you to do."

Balaam didn't wait to hear from God before he went with the Moabite leaders, which made God very angry – and as Balaam rode along on his donkey, the angel of the Lord stood in his path.

When the donkey saw the angel holding a sword, it turned into a field. So Balaam beat his donkey.

Then the donkey saw the angel a second time – and moved over against a wall, crushing Balaam's foot. Again Balaam beat the donkey.

When the donkey saw the angel for a third time, it lay down. So Balaam beat it with a stick!

Then God allowed Balaam to see the angel.

"Why did you beat your donkey three times?" asked the angel. "I have come to bar your way because you should not be making this journey. But your donkey saw me and turned aside three times. If it had not done so, I would have killed you."

Balaam realized what a fool he had been. When he met with Balak, he did as God told him and blessed the Israelites instead of cursing them.

The Death of Moses

Deuteronomy 32:48 "Go to the Abarim Mountains in the land of Moab opposite the city of Jericho; climb Mount Nebo and look at the land of Canaan that I am about to give the people of Israel."

When God told Moses that He would not allow him to lead the Israelites into the Promised Land, Moses accepted God's word.

As time passed, everyone who had left Egypt died except Caleb, Joshua, and Moses; apart from them, only those who were born in the desert survived.

Moses told the Israelites' new leader, Joshua, that the Lord would never leave him. Then he gave his blessing to all the tribes of Israel – and walked to the top of the highest mountain, as God had commanded.

"This is the land I promised Abraham, Isaac, and Jacob," said God, as Moses looked out over all of Canaan. "You disobeyed me when you were at the waters of Meribah – and struck the rock with the stick. Because of this, I will let you see everything, but I will not allow you to cross over the Jordan River."

Moses was one hundred and twenty years old when he died at the top of that mountain, but he could still see Canaan as well as anyone.

Did you know?

God himself buried Moses in a valley in Moab, but no one knows exactly where.

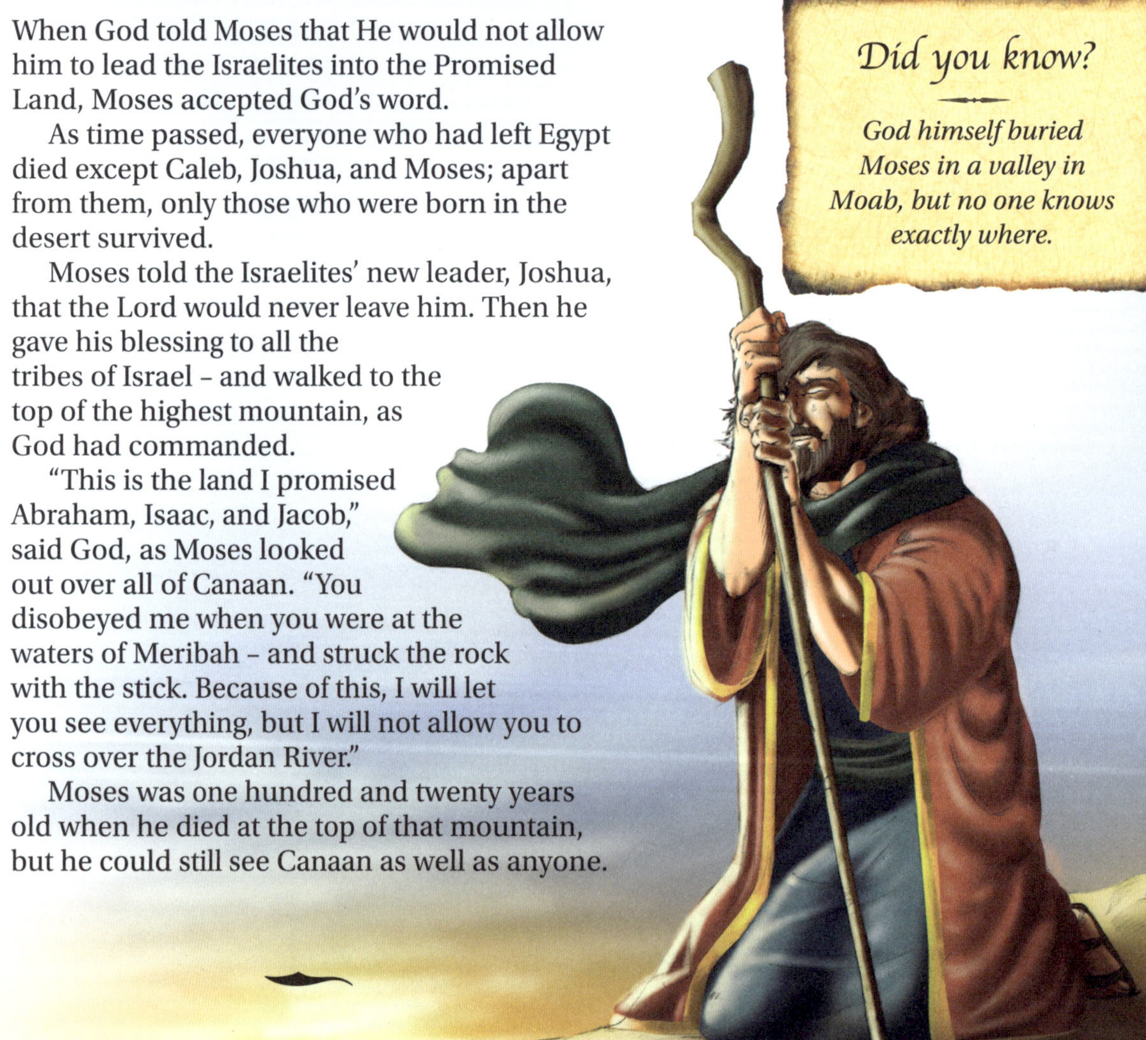

Rahab and the Spies

Joshua 2:1 Then Joshua sent two spies from the camp at Acacia with orders to go and secretly explore the land of Canaan, especially the city of Jericho.

Before Joshua led his people into Canaan, the Promised Land, he sent two of his most trusted men across the Jordan River to spy on Jericho, the largest city in Canaan.

The spies hid at the home of a woman named Rahab, who lived in a house built into the walls of the city. But the king of Jericho soon learned that the Israelites were there and sent men to capture them.

Thinking quickly, Rahab hid the spies on the roof of her house until the soldiers had left. Then she said, "I know that God has given this land to the Israelites. We have heard how your God helped you cross the Red Sea, so promise me that my family and I will be safe when you conquer the city."

"You have saved our lives - and we will save yours," replied Joshua's men. "But you must tell no one that we have been here."

Rahab lowered the two spies from her window with a rope, and they ran off into the night. But before they left, the men told Rahab to hang a red cord from her window, so that the Israelites would know which house was hers when they invaded the city.

Crossing the Jordan

Joshua 3:10-11 "You will know that the living God is among you when the Covenant Box of the Lord of all the earth crosses the Jordan ahead of you."

To reach Canaan, the Israelites first had to cross the Jordan River. Now that Moses was dead, Joshua was the people's leader, and it was his job to guide everyone safely across.

Now Canaan was a dangerous place, so, before his people crossed the river, Joshua had sent two of his bravest men ahead to spy on the land. Joshua wanted to know all he could about Canaan, especially Jericho, which was the largest city.

At last, the day came when God's chosen people, the Israelites, were to cross the Jordan River.

There was no bridge across the vast river, but following God's instructions, Joshua told the priests what to do.

Carrying the Ark of the Covenant, which contained God's laws, the Ten Commandments, the priests walked up to the river and stepped into the water.

As the people watched, the water level fell. Upstream, the riverbanks collapsed, blocking the whole stream, and the water began to pile up. But near Jericho, where they stood, the Israelites were able to walk across the riverbed – and into the Promised Land.

The Walls of Jericho

Joshua 6:21 With their swords, they killed everyone in the city, men and women, young and old. They also killed the cattle, sheep, and donkeys.

The gates of Jericho, with its huge stone walls, were guarded to keep the Israelites out. But God told Joshua that for six days, he

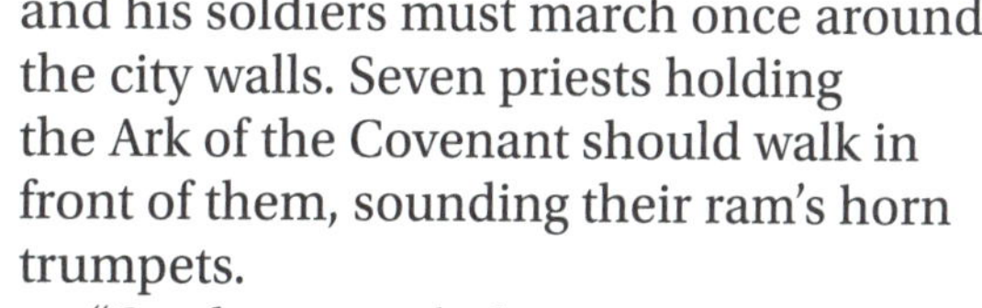

and his soldiers must march once around the city walls. Seven priests holding the Ark of the Covenant should walk in front of them, sounding their ram's horn trumpets.

"On the seventh day, you must march around the city seven times," said God. "Then, when the trumpets sound, tell all the Israelites to shout at the tops of their voices."

The people of Jericho watched with curiosity as the Israelites marched around outside their city walls each day, blowing their trumpets. "What are these people doing?" they wondered.

On the seventh day, Joshua cried, "Today, Jericho is yours!" And as the final trumpet blew, thousands upon thousands of Israelites began to shout louder and louder.

The people of Jericho looked terrified as the walls began to crack. Stones crumbled, towers fell – and the walls of Jericho came down! "The city of Jericho is ours!" cheered the Israelites.

Gibeon Tricks Joshua

Joshua 9:1 The victories of Israel became known to all the kings west of the Jordan – in the hills, in the foothills, and all along the coastal plain of the Mediterranean Sea as far north as Lebanon.

When they heard how the Israelites had conquered Jericho and Ai, the other tribes in Canaan became very afraid, so they all came together to fight against the Israelites.

But the Gibeonites decided to trick Joshua and sent a group of men, wearing old, ragged clothes and sandals to talk to him.

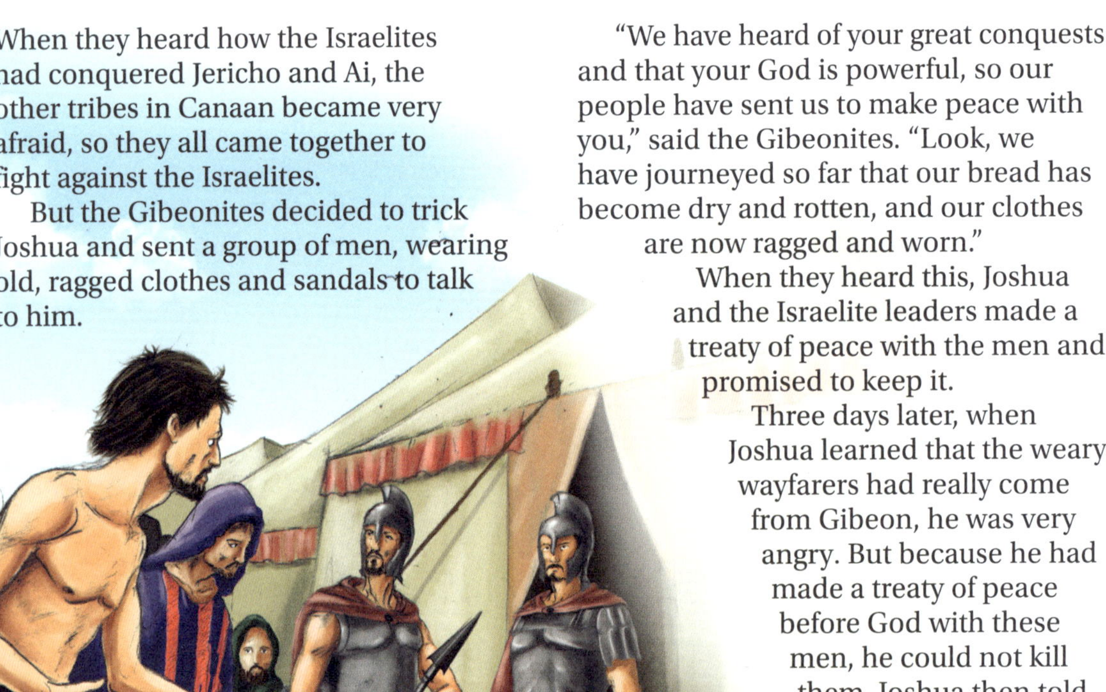

"We have heard of your great conquests and that your God is powerful, so our people have sent us to make peace with you," said the Gibeonites. "Look, we have journeyed so far that our bread has become dry and rotten, and our clothes are now ragged and worn."

When they heard this, Joshua and the Israelite leaders made a treaty of peace with the men and promised to keep it.

Three days later, when Joshua learned that the weary wayfarers had really come from Gibeon, he was very angry. But because he had made a treaty of peace before God with these men, he could not kill them. Joshua then told the Gibeonites that because they had deceived him, God would condemn all their people to be slaves.

Joshua Divides the Land

Joshua 23:10 "Any one of you can make a thousand men run away, because the Lord your God is fighting for you, just as He promised."

Time passed, and the Israelites fought and won many battles. With each passing year, they accumulated more and more land.

By this time, Joshua was very old and knew that he would die soon.

Now, there were twelve tribes, each descended from Jacob's sons, and Joshua fairly divided the land between all of them.

Then Joshua told the leaders that if they obeyed the Lord at all times, He would give them victory in every battle they fought, and all the remaining land would become theirs. "But if you turn away from God or worship false gods or idols, God will take away everything He has given to you," said Joshua.

The leaders cried, "We will always worship and serve the one, true God!"

Then he told all the other Israelites the same thing: "Turn away from idols made of wood and stone, and obey God always!"

"We will!" chorused the people. "There is only one true God!"

But as much as he loved his people, Joshua knew they could sometimes be weak and greedy and forget to obey God's commands.

Did you know?

Joshua died soon after making this speech to his people. He was one hundred and ten years old.

The Tribes and the Altar

Joshua 22:34 The people of Reuben and Gad said, "This altar is a witness to all of us that the Lord is God." And so they named it "Witness."

One day, Joshua called for the people of the tribes of Reuben, Gad, and East Manasseh to listen to a message.

"You have always obeyed the Lord and served him well," Joshua told them. "Because of this, I am sending you back to your home with my blessing."

So, leaving the other Israelites in Canaan, on the west of the Jordan, the tribes of Reuben, Gad, and East Manasseh began their journey back to Gilead, on the east side of the Jordan.

On their way, the tribes stopped to build a large altar in a place called Geliloth. When the people of Israel heard this, they were furious - and declared war! "How dare these tribes from the east build an altar on our side of the Jordan!" they said.

Phinehas, the son of Eleazar the priest, went to the tribes of Reuben, Gad, and East Manasseh and said, "You have rebelled against the Lord by building your own altar to burn offerings on, and now God will be angry with all Israelites!"

But the tribes told Phinehas that they had not built the altar for themselves, but so that their descendants in Canaan would see the altar and know that they, the tribes of Reuben, Gad, and East Manasseh praised God.

When Phinehas heard this, he was satisfied and so were the people of Israel, who called off their war.

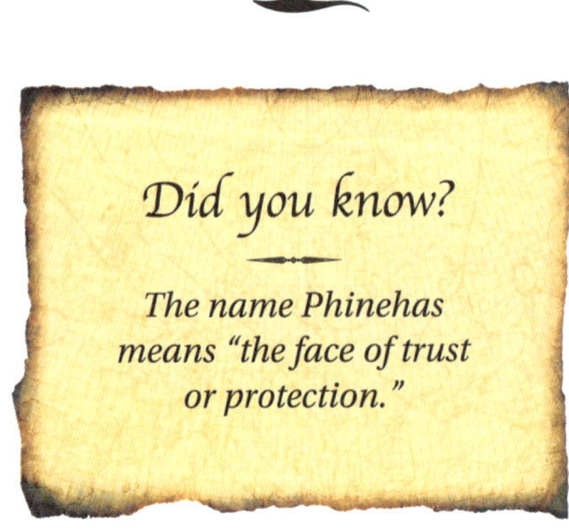

Did you know?

The name Phinehas means "the face of trust or protection."

Deborah and Jael

Judges 4:9 She answered, "All right, I will go with you, but you won't get any credit for the victory because the Lord will hand Sisera over to a woman."

Now that Joshua was dead, the Israelites became weak and forgot about God. But God never stopped loving them and sometimes sent brave leaders, known as "judges," to help them give up their disobedient ways.

One such judge was Deborah. God sent her to help the Israelites, who were being invaded by the Canaanites. Jabin, their king, had a great number of soldiers, who were led by a general named Sisera.

Once a mighty force, the Israelites were now too afraid to fight against Sisera, so Deborah sent for an Israelite named Barak and told him, "You must take ten thousand soldiers to Mount Tabor. I will bring Sisera to fight you at the Kishon River, but you shall have victory over them!"

But Barak wouldn't go without Deborah in the lead. This annoyed Deborah, who told him, "Very well, I'll come along – but don't think everyone will praise you as the hero of the battle. God has told me that Sisera will be killed by a woman."

The Israelites won the battle, just as Deborah had predicted, and only Sisera escaped. He ran into the tent of a woman named Jael, who agreed to hide him. But as soon as Sisera fell asleep, Jael killed him with a tent peg. Just as Deborah had said, he died at the hands of a woman.

Did you know?

There are four other female prophetesses in the Old Testament: Miriam, Huldah, Noadiah, and Isiah's unnamed wife.

God Comes to Gideon

Judges 7:21 Every man stood in his place around the camp, and the whole enemy army ran away yelling.

The Israelites had a powerful enemy called the Midianites. These people were fierce tribesmen who swooped in after the harvest, burning wheat and stealing grapes, olives, and animals.

After seven years, the Israelites were in despair. Then God sent an angel to a young farmer named Gideon.

"You must save your people!" the angel told him.

"But I am only a poor and humble farmer," said Gideon.

"The Lord will be with you," the angel reassured him.

When Gideon had gathered an army of men, God said, "Take them to the stream to drink water. Keep with you those who lap the water like dogs, but send away any others."

When darkness fell, Gideon gave each of the three hundred men who had lapped the water a ram's horn trumpet and a flaming torch covered by an earthenware jar. Silently, the Israelite army surrounded the Midianites' camp. Then on Gideon's signal, they loudly blew their trumpets, smashed their jars to reveal their torchlight, and shouted as loud as they could. Confused and terrified, the Midianites began fighting with each other as they fled into the night. God had helped Gideon to drive the enemy away.

Jotham and Abimelech

Judges 9:6 Then all the men of Shechem and Bethmillo got together and went to the sacred oak tree at Shechem, where they made Abimelech king.

Gideon had seventy sons by his many wives, including Abimelech, his son by a young servant girl.

After Gideon's death, Abimelech feared that his half-brothers would rule the land. So, helped by his mother's relatives, who lived in a town named Shechem, Abimelech hired a group of thugs and ruffians to help him.

Then Abimelech and his followers went to his father's home and killed all his brothers, except one: Gideon's youngest son, Jotham, managed to hide. Then the men of Shechem and Bethmillo made Abimelech their king.

When Jotham heard that Abimelech had been made king, he told the people of Shechem a story: "Long ago, all the trees tried to choose a king for themselves.

"'To govern you, I would have to stop producing my oil, which is used to praise the gods and men,' said the olive tree.

"'I would have to stop producing my delicious fruit,' said the fig tree.

"'I would have to stop producing my sweet-tasting wine,' said the grapevine.

"Only the sharp, prickly thorn bush wanted to rule the trees. It threatened the others, saying, 'If you want to make me your king, then come and take shelter in my shade. If you don't, fire will blaze from my thorny branches and burn up all the trees that don't do as I say.'"

Jotham was trying to tell the people that they had not chosen their king wisely – and that a man like Abimelech could rule only by threats and treacherous violence.

After Abimelech had been king for three years, the people rebelled against him and killed him.

Samson and the Lion

Judges 14:8 On the way, he left the road to look at the lion he had killed, and he was surprised to find a swarm of bees and some honey inside the dead body.

A childless Israelite couple were visited by an angel who told them that they would have a son who would win a great victory over the Israelites' enemy, the Philistines. "But you must never cut his hair," warned the angel. The child was named Samson, and he grew tall and strong.

Years later, Samson fell in love with a Philistine woman. His parents wanted him to be happy, so they agreed he could marry her. While they were on their way to visit the girl, Samson was attacked by a lion. But God had given him such great strength that he killed the lion with his bare hands.

Some days later, on the way to his wedding, Samson noticed that bees had built a nest in the lion's body. On the first day of the wedding celebrations, Samson asked the Philistine guests a riddle. To the person who solved it, he would give them thirty changes of fine new clothing. He told them:

"Out of the eater came something to eat, and out of the strong came something sweet."

The Philistines threatened to kill Samson's bride unless she told them the answer to Samson's riddle. So she pestered him until he gave her the answer. That night, the men said to Samson, "What's sweeter than honey and stronger than a lion?"

Realizing that his wife had betrayed him, Samson returned to his parents' house and never saw her again – and he fought the Philistines as his mortal enemies for the rest of his life.

Did you know?
In Hebrew, the name
Samson means "sun child"
or "bright sun."

Samson and Delilah

Judges 16:17 Samson told Delilah, "My hair has never been cut. I have been dedicated to God as a Nazarite since the day I was born."

Samson was a Nazarite, which is a person dedicated to God. As such, Samson never cut his hair and often wore it braided.

After leaving his first wife, Samson eventually fell in love with another woman, whose name was Delilah. Some Philistines offered to pay her a huge sum of money if she uncovered the secret of Samson's strength.

Delilah, who was very greedy, repeatedly asked Samson what made him so strong. Each time she asked, Samson made up an answer. But none of his stories were true. At last, Samson gave in to his wife and told her the true answer. "If my hair is cut, my strength will be lost," he said. Of course, Delilah told the Philistines.

That night, when Samson fell asleep, one of the Philistines crept in and cut off his hair. Samson, now weakened, was soon overpowered. The Philistines blinded him and chained him in prison. But then his hair began to grow back.

The Philistines had a great feast in a temple to celebrate their victory over Samson. "Bring Samson here!" they laughed. The temple was crowded and everyone was mocking Samson.

"Dear Lord," he prayed, "please give me strength just one more time."

Samson stretched out his arms and pushed against the pillars holding up the temple, and the whole building crashed down, killing everyone, including Samson.

Ruth and Boaz

Ruth 1:16 But Ruth answered, "Don't ask me to leave you! Let me go with you. Wherever you go, I will go; wherever you live, I will live."

Naomi lived in a place called Moab for several years. Her husband and both her sons had died there, and she now lived with her sons' two widows, Orpah and Ruth. However, Naomi longed to return to Bethlehem, where she had lived when she was a child.

"We'll come with you," said her daughters-in-law. "No," said Naomi. "Go back to your families or marry again." Orpah returned to her family, but Ruth decided to go with Naomi.

They arrived in Bethlehem at harvest time. In those days, women were not allowed to earn a living, but the law said that the poor could go into fields and gather stray stalks of grain that had been dropped and keep them for themselves. So Ruth went to a local farm and gathered barley.

The farm belonged to Boaz, a wealthy farmer. "What a kind girl to look after her mother-in-law," he said to his farm workers. "Pull some barley from your bundles and leave it for her." That evening, Ruth brought home a huge bundle of barley to grind into flour and bake fresh bread.

Naomi was delighted to hear which farm Ruth had worked on. "Boaz is my nearest relation," she said. "Perhaps he'll help us. Go back there tomorrow."

So throughout the harvest, Ruth returned to the same field. Soon Boaz fell in love with her. At the end of the harvest, Ruth and Boaz married, and the next year they had a son.

Hannah's Son

1 Samuel 3:8-9 Then Eli understood that it was the Lord calling the child.

Elkanah had two wives, Peninnah and Hannah. Peninnah, who had children, teased Hannah because she had none. One night, Hannah went to the temple and prayed to God, "Please send me a son, and I promise to devote his life to your service."

Eli, the high priest, blessed her as she left. "May God grant your wish," he said.

Some time later, Hannah gave birth to a son named Samuel. Remembering her promise to God, she took Samuel to the temple and gave him to Eli to look after.

Every year, Hannah visited Samuel and gave him a new coat. The boy grew up to be as honest as Eli's own sons were dishonest.

One night, Samuel heard someone call him. He jumped up and ran to Eli. "I didn't call you," said the old man.

Three times Samuel heard the voice, and finally, Eli told him, "It must be the voice of God that you heard. If He calls you again, say 'speak to me, Lord. Your servant is listening.'" So this time Samuel listened.

"Tell Eli that I shall punish his sons because they have turned against me," said God.

The next morning, when Samuel told Eli what God had said, Eli sadly replied, "He is God. He must do what is right." Soon after, Eli's sons were killed in battle by the Philistines.

God Visits Samuel

1 Samuel 8:18 "When that time comes, you will complain bitterly because of your king, whom you yourselves chose, but the Lord will not listen to your complaints."

Soon after God had spoken to Samuel, the Philistines attacked the Israelites and defeated them in a terrible battle. Some Israelites had the idea to take the gold Covenant Chest with them to the battlefield, to show their enemies that God was with them. Eli's sons carried the chest to the army camp.

When the soldiers on the battlefield saw the chest, they cheered loudly. The Philistines then fought even harder. They defeated the Israelites, killed Eli's sons, and carried off the Covenant Chest in triumph.

By now, Eli was old and nearly blind. When he heard that his sons were dead and the sacred box had been taken, he fell to the floor and died.

But wherever the chest went, disease and plague spread. Fearfully, the Philistines put the chest on a wooden cart, piled gifts of gold all around it, and sent it back to Israel. No sooner had the Israelites received their chest back, than the Philistines began attacking them again. Samuel, who was now a respected adult, gathered the Israelites together. "God will only rescue you from Philistine persecution if you stop praising other gods," he said.

The people did as Samuel said. By following God's ways, they grew strong against the Philistines and won back all the cities that had been captured. Samuel helped and advised anyone in need. Being so close to God, he was a fair and honest judge.

Years later, when Samuel grew old, people began discussing what they would do when he died. They invited him to a meeting and said they wanted a king. Samuel was sad and felt that the Israelites no longer wanted him. Samuel told God how he felt.

"They are refusing me as their leader, not you, Samuel. They don't want me to lead them anymore," God replied.

So Samuel called everyone together once again. "If you have a king," he warned, "he will take all that is yours for himself. He will make your sons fight in his armies and your daughters work in his palace. He will take your land."

"But we want a king!" repeated the people. They imagined a wonderful man who would make their lives even better. "Let them have what they ask for," God told Samuel. "You will have your king soon," Samuel told the Israelites.

Saul Becomes King of Israel

1 Samuel 10:24 Samuel said to the people, "Here is the man the Lord has chosen! There is no one else among us like him."

When Samuel, the leader of the Israelites, grew old, God said to him, "A man of the tribe of Benjamin will come to you. He will be king. You will know him when you see him."

Soon after this, a tall young man named Saul approached Samuel outside the city. "I've lost three of my donkeys," he said. "I know you are a prophet. Can you tell me where they are?"

"Your donkeys are safe," replied Samuel, "but you must come with me because you are going to be the first king of Israel."

"But I'm not that important! I come from the smallest tribe in Israel," replied Saul.

Smiling, Samuel took a little flask of olive oil and sprinkled a few drops on Saul's head. This was a sign that God had chosen him.

Later, Samuel planned to present Saul to the people. But when a huge crowd of Israelites gathered, Saul hid out of view.

When the Israelites finally coaxed him out, Saul stood head and shoulders above everyone.

"Long live King Saul! God save the King!" cried the Israelites.

Then Samuel listed Saul's duties as king, which included doing what God said and not just what he wanted to do.

Saul Forgets God

1 Samuel 13:13 And Samuel said to Saul, "You have been foolish; you have not kept God's commandment. Now your kingdom will be ruled by others forever."

Not everyone rejoiced at Saul being made king. "Who does he think he is?" grumbled some of the Israelites.

Meanwhile, another enemy, the Ammonites, attacked the town of Jabesh. The Israelites sent an urgent message to Saul, who immediately summoned his army and attacked the Ammonites early the next morning. By noon, the Ammonite army had been defeated. The Israelites were overjoyed and wanted to kill everyone who hadn't wanted Saul to be king, but he told them that there would be no more killing on this day of victory. The Israelites all felt happy that Saul had proved his ability to be king.

Two years later, thousands of Philistines gathered on the border of Israel, preparing for invasion. Samuel told Saul to wait for seven days and then together they would offer a sacrifice to God. But after seven days had passed, Samuel had not returned, and Saul grew impatient and made the sacrifice himself.

When Samuel returned, he asked, "Why have you disobeyed me?"

"Because you didn't come, the Philistines may attack at any moment, and I was worried that if I didn't offer the sacrifice, we would be defeated," explained Saul.

"You have disobeyed God!" said Samuel. "Because you went against his word, your sons will not succeed you – and another family, not your own, will rule Israel."

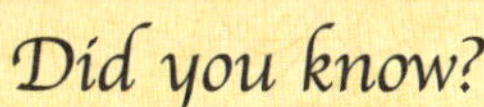

Did you know?

Every one of Saul's men, including his three sons, was killed in battle on Mount Gilboa.

David and Goliath

1 Samuel 17:32-33 "Do not lose heart, sir. I will go and fight this Philistine." Saul answered, "You cannot go and fight with this Philistine, you are only a boy, and he has been a fighting man all his life."

God told Samuel to go to Bethlehem and find a man named Jesse. "One of his sons will be the next king."

In Bethlehem, people lined up for Samuel to bless them, as he was now a great and powerful man. All seven of Jesse's sons came to be blessed, and Samuel wondered which of the tall, handsome men God had chosen. But as he blessed each one, God said, "Don't look at their faces – just look into their hearts."

Finally, Samuel turned to Jesse and asked, "Are all your children here?"

Jesse replied, "My youngest, David, is in the fields looking after the sheep."

"Please fetch him," said Samuel.

When the boy appeared, God said, "This is the one."

Meanwhile, Saul and the Israelites were at war with the Philistines. One morning, a man named Goliath marched out of the Philistine army and stood before the Israelites. He was the tallest and strongest man anyone had ever seen.

"Choose someone from among you to fight me," he bellowed to the Israelites. "If he kills me, the Philistines will be your servants. But if I win, you will be our servants." Saul and his army were worried. Who could fight such a man and win?

David was sent to the Israelites' camp by his father with food for three of his brothers who were in Saul's army. As he arrived, Goliath declared his challenge again.

"Goliath is not stronger than God," said David. "I will fight him!"

Saul overheard this and said, "Goliath is a powerful soldier. What makes you think you could win?"

"I may be young," said David, "but with God's help I have killed lions and bears that have attacked my sheep. God will help me now."

Refusing both weapons and shield, David, who was already carrying his slingshot, picked up five smooth stones. He walked toward Goliath.

"Get out of my way, boy!" roared Goliath. "I don't fight children!"

"You come with sword and spear," David shouted back, "but I come with God, who is stronger than you and your army!"

Furious, Goliath strode toward David, who put a stone in his slingshot and hurled it at him. The stone hit Goliath's forehead and sank in, causing the giant to fall. When the Philistines saw that Goliath was dead, they fled from the battlefield.

Did you know?

Shepherds used to carry a slingshot at all times to throw stones at animals that threatened sheep.

Jonathan Saves David

1 Samuel 24:17-18 He said to David, "You are more righteous than I am, as you have treated me well even though I have treated you very badly."

Saul was so delighted with David that he gave him command of the army and took him to live in his own house. Saul's son, Jonathan, loved David like a brother and shared all his expensive clothes and belongings with him. Saul's daughter, Michal, married David, and the Israelites treated him as their hero.

But over time, Saul grew so jealous of David that one day, he threw a spear at his head. Fortunately, David dodged the spear and escaped. Jonathan spoke to his father to defend David, but it was no use. Saul hated David.

The next day, Jonathan warned David that Saul was still trying to kill him and advised his friend to go into the wilderness and hide.

One day, Saul stepped into a cave where David was hiding. David saw and crept up behind him, then cut off a piece of his coat. When Saul had left the cave, David called to him, "My King, it is I, David. See how close I came to killing you, and yet I spared your life! I wouldn't harm someone who has been anointed by God."

Ashamed, Saul replied, "David, I have treated you badly, but you are greater than I. Long may you reign as the future king of Israel. But promise me that, when you are king, you will treat my family well."

David promised that he would.

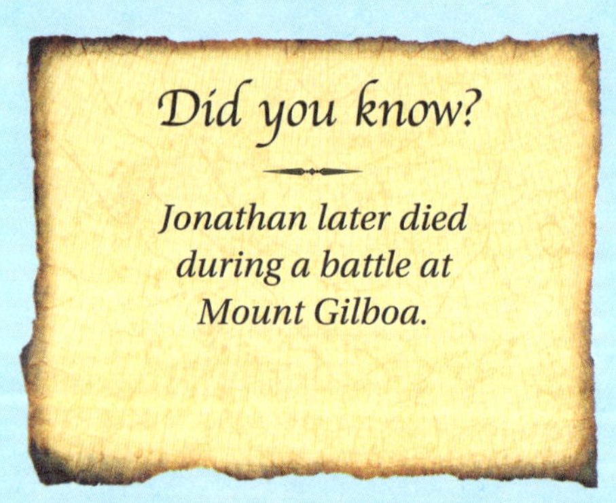

David and Abigail

1 Samuel 25:32 And David said to Abigail, "Blessed be the Lord, the God of Israel, who sent you to meet me today!"

While David and his followers were hiding from Saul in the wilderness, it was very difficult to find any food. So when a wealthy farmer named Nabal gave a feast, David sent some messengers to him.

"We would be grateful for any food you can spare," they said.

But Nabal was scornful. "I've never heard of David, and I'm not giving away good food to a group of beggars!" he told them.

When David heard about this, he was furious. "Fetch your swords!" he said. "We will show Nabal who we are!"

But Nabal's wife, Abigail, who was a kind young woman, was distressed by her husband's meanness. Secretly, she loaded five donkeys with fruit, fresh bread, fig cakes, meat, and wine, and rode with them to find David.

When Abigail saw him, she begged for his mercy. "Please don't take revenge because of what my foolish husband said!" she pleaded.

David promised Abigail that he would leave Nabal unharmed.

When Abigail returned to home, Nabal was holding a feast and was drunk. When she told him the next morning that she had met with David, his heart failed him and he died ten days later.

Later, Abigail married David.

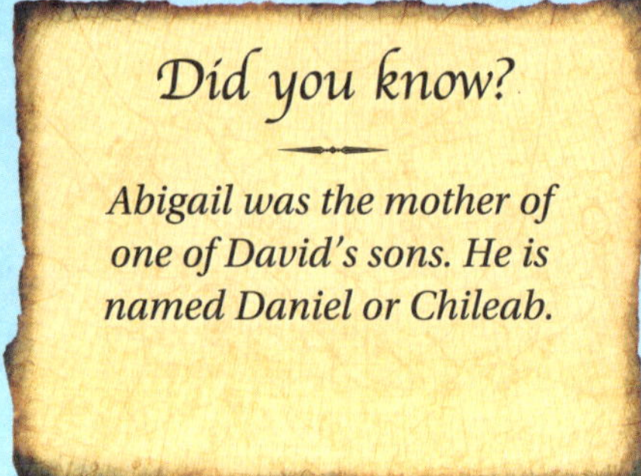

Did you know?

Abigail was the mother of one of David's sons. He is named Daniel or Chileab.

King David

2 Samuel 6:21 "I was dancing to praise the Lord, who chose me, instead of your father and his family, to make me the leader of his people in Israel."

When Samuel died, everyone mourned. The Philistines were preparing for another battle, and Saul felt powerless. In desperation, he visited a witch who claimed she could speak to the dead. Since witchcraft was forbidden, Saul went in disguise. "Ask Samuel what will happen," he said.

"I see a man dressed in a cloak," the witch replied.

Then Samuel's voice spoke: "God has left you. Tomorrow, the Philistines will be victorious, and you and your sons will die."

Sure enough, the following day, the Philistines won the battle and Saul, Jonathan, and Saul's other sons all died, just as Samuel had foretold.

David was welcomed as king in the city of Hebron. Some years later, he led the Israelites to Jerusalem, which would be their new capital. But the people of Jerusalem would not let them in, so some Israelites climbed a water shaft and unlocked the gates. Then they all rushed in and captured the city.

Later, a huge procession followed priests carrying the Ark of the Covenant into Jerusalem. David was so happy that he danced with his people. His wife Michal scolded, "You behaved like a fool!"

"Nothing I do to glorify God is wrong!" replied David. "In fact, I'm going to build a temple for God here."

Did you know?

David had eight wives: Michal, Ahinoam, Abigail, Maachah, Haggith, Abital, Eglah, and Bathsheba.

David and Bathsheba

2 Samuel 12:13-14 "The Lord forgives you, you will not die. But because you have shown such contempt for the Lord in doing this, your child will die."

One evening, from the roof of his palace, David saw a beautiful woman bathing in the river.

"Her name is Bathsheba," a messenger told him. "She is the wife of Uriah, one of your soldiers who is away at war."

Like most kings of that time, David had several wives, but he now also wanted to marry Bathsheba. He sent a secret order to Uriah's commanding officer to put Uriah in the front line, where the fighting was fiercest.

Before long, news came that Uriah had been killed, just as David had wanted. David married Bathsheba, who soon gave birth to a son.

God was angry and sent a prophet named Nathan to show David how cruel he had been to Uriah.

Nathan told David a story. "There were two men. One was rich, with many animals, and the other was poor, his only possession a little lamb that he loved dearly. A visitor arrived at the rich man's house and asked for food. Not wanting to lose any of his own animals, the rich man had the poor man's lamb killed and cooked."

David was horrified. "The rich man should be punished!"

"But you are like the rich man," said Nathan. "And you will be punished. Because of what you have done, your son will die!"

Did you know?

In Hebrew, the name Bathsheba means "daughter of oath."

Absalom Rebels

2 Samuel 18:17 They took Absalom's body, threw it into a deep pit in the forest, and covered it with a huge pile of stones.

King David had many children, but they were all envious of each other. Who would David choose as the next king? One of his sons, Absalom, fought and killed his half-brother, David's eldest son. Absalom fled, but two years later, he returned to Jerusalem.

Absalom was very proud of his long hair. He was also determined to be the next king, so he made himself popular with the people before going to Hebron and raising an army. Then he challenged his father to battle.

David rode out of Jerusalem leading thousands of men, but he gave instructions to the commanders to be gentle with Absalom.

After a long battle, Absalom and his men escaped. Absalom leapt on a donkey, which bolted through the woods, but his hair got caught on the branches of a tree, and he was left dangling helplessly. When Joab, the commander of the army, heard about this news, he rode with his soldiers to where Absalom was still dangling and they killed him.

When David was told of Absalom's death, he was overcome with grief. "My son!" he wept. "If only I had been killed instead of you!"

David Chooses Solomon

1 Kings 1:39 There, Zadok the priest took the horn of oil from the tent and anointed Solomon. Then they blew the trumpet, and all the people said, "Long live King Solomon!"

When King David was old, he stayed in bed. Outside his room, people discussed who would be the next king. Now that Absalom was dead, Adonijah was David's eldest surviving son. He was handsome and ambitious, and he had made up his mind to be crowned immediately.

Adonijah held a feast and declared himself king but did not invite Solomon, who was Bathsheba's second son. As soon as Bathsheba heard about it, she rushed to tell David, "You once promised that our son, Solomon, would be king after you," she said. "Everyone is longing to know who will be king, and now Adonijah is telling everyone that he is to be the next king."

Nathan the prophet was there, too. "It's true," he told David. "The people are all shouting 'Long live King Adonijah'!"

"Adonijah is not my choice!" said David. "Solomon will be the next king. Put him on my mule and lead him through the city. Let the High Priest anoint him with oil, then blow the trumpet and bring him back in triumph."

When Adonijah heard the people outside the palace cheering for King Solomon, he knew his plot had failed. King David had chosen Solomon to be the next king of Israel.

Solomon's Wish

1 Kings 3:11 "Because you have asked for the wisdom to rule justly, instead of long life for yourself, riches, or the death of your enemies, I will do what you have asked."

When King David was dying, he spoke to Solomon, "Soon I will not be here to advise you. Be strong and remember to always obey God."

After David died, Solomon became king and married the daughter of the king of Egypt. He tried to do what God wanted, but he was worried about ruling the people of Israel on his own. Solomon often prayed to God for advice, and one night God spoke to him in a dream.

"Tell me what you want," said God.

Solomon replied, "You have made me the king of a great people, but I have no idea how to govern them. Please give me wisdom."

God was pleased and answered, "Because you asked for nothing for yourself, I will grant your wish. If you obey my laws, you will be the wisest king that ever lived. I will also give you things you did not ask for. You will be rich and respected by everyone, and you will have a long life."

Solomon knew that it was a dream, but he also knew that God had really spoken to him, so he threw a party to celebrate God's promise to him.

The Wise King

1 Kings 3:28 When the people of Israel heard of Solomon's decision, they were filled with respect for him, because they knew then that God had give him the wisdom to settle disputes fairly.

God granted Solomon's wish. He became very wise, and many people brought their problems to him so that he could solve them.

One day, two unhappy women came to see Solomon. One of the women carried a baby.

"Your Majesty," one woman began, "we live in a house together."

The other woman added. "We've both just had babies within two days of each other."

"Last night," continued the first woman, "this woman's baby died, and she took my baby while I was asleep and left her dead baby in its place!"

"That's not true!" wailed the second woman. "This is my baby!"

The two women began arguing, and King Solomon let them continue for a while. Then he said, "Bring me my sword!" The sword was brought to Solomon, and he commanded, "Cut the child in two!"

"That seems fair," said one woman.

"No! Don't kill my baby! I would rather give him away than have you kill him!" sobbed the second woman.

Solomon smiled, "The mother of this child is the one who wants to spare his life. Give the baby to her!"

Such tales of Solomon's wisdom spread far and wide across the world.

Solomon's Temple

1 Kings 8:65 There at the Temple, Solomon and all the people of Israel celebrated the Festival of Shelters for seven days.

In the fourth year of Solomon's reign, he began to build a wonderful temple for God. Large stones and strong woods such as cedar were used for the foundations and walls. The best cedar trees grew in a place named Tyre, so Solomon made a treaty with Hiram, the king of Tyre. Once cut, the wood was tied together in rafts and floated down the coast, close to where Solomon was building the Temple. In return, Solomon supplied Tyre with wheat and olive oil.

The Temple would be a wonderful place where the Ark of the Covenant would be kept in a special room. The room, which was at the back of the temple, was windowless, with floors and walls covered in gold. It was decorated with carved figures of winged creatures, palm trees, and flowers, also covered in gold.

The outer room had a gold altar and ten golden lamp stands. The tables, cups, and bowls - even the pans that were used to carry coal to the fires - were made of glistening gold, and outside the Temple there were beautiful courtyards.

Thousands of men worked on the Temple over seven years. When it was finished, Solomon held a special opening ceremony, where priests carried the Ark of the Covenant inside. Then they had a great celebration, which lasted for a week.

The Queen of Sheba Visits

1 Kings 10:1 The queen of Sheba heard of Solomon's fame, and she journeyed to Jerusalem to test him with difficult questions.

The Queen of Sheba lived in a southern kingdom at the other end of the ancient trade routes. When she heard about Solomon, the queen decided to see for herself how wise he was.

The queen wrote a list of difficult questions for Solomon. Then, taking jewels, gold, and spices, she set out for Jerusalem. When she arrived at Solomon's palace, the queen was shown into his throne room.

"All these gifts are for you," the queen told Solomon. "Now let me ask you some questions."

"Ask me anything you like," said Solomon.

The queen was amazed to find that Solomon was able to answer every question she asked, and he explained to her everything she had ever wondered about. "All I have heard about you is true!" she exclaimed. "You are wiser and richer than I thought could be possible. How lucky your people are to have you as their king!"

Then Solomon gave the queen as many rich gifts as she had given him.

"I can see that God has given Israel a wonderful king," said the queen, as she returned to her home across the desert.

Solomon's Sins

1 Kings 11:3 Solomon married seven hundred princesses and also had three hundred concubines. They made him turn away from God.

During Solomon's reign, Israel flourished. Beautiful buildings and great cities were built. But to pay for it all, people had to pay taxes, and men had to work for the king rather than for themselves. For Solomon's navy to be successful, sailors had to leave their homes and families for years to travel to other countries, in order to bring back riches for Solomon. Some never returned, perishing at sea. So money poured into Solomon's treasury each year, but he continued to spend far more than he received. Many Israelites became poor and unhappy.

Solomon also married princesses from other countries, who praised their own gods. It helped to keep peace between lands because his wives' fathers wouldn't fight with their son-in-law, and it was good for trade. But it also brought problems, as the wives tempted Solomon to worship their own gods and goddesses.

God was upset. He longed to see Solomon following Him as David had done.

"Solomon," God said, "I promised to give you the kingdom of Israel, and you promised to obey me. You have broken your part of the bargain. Although I should take the kingdom away from you, because of my vow to your father, David, I will leave a small part of the kingdom for your family to rule after you die. But the rest will be given to someone else."

Ahab and Jezebel

1 Kings 16:32 He built a temple to Baal in Samaria, made an altar for him, and put it in the temple.

After Solomon's death, Israel was divided in two. In the south, Judah was ruled by Solomon's son, Rehoboam. In the north, Jeroboam ruled. He was a young man whom Solomon had trusted very much.

None of the kings after Jeroboam were faithful to God. One king, Ahab, sinned against God more than any of his predecessors. He married a woman named Jezebel, who had been princess of the nearby country of Phoenicia.

Jezebel praised a god named Baal and was determined to put a stop to the worship of Israel's God. She believed that kings and queens could make up their own laws, and she had as many Jewish prophets executed as she could.

Ahab and Jezebel lived in the new capital city of Samaria, built by Ahab's father. It had a grand palace, and they built a temple to Baal. They also built a royal villa overlooking rolling hills and lush vineyards. Adjoining it was a vineyard owned by a man named Naboth. Ahab wanted this vineyard, but Naboth didn't want to sell it to him.

So Jezebel took matters into her own hands. Using false evidence, she had Naboth and his sons accused of treason, and they were found guilty and executed. After they had died, Jezebel told Ahab the vineyard was his.

Their unfair treatment of Naboth made a lot of people hate Ahab and Jezebel, and later, God punished both of them for their evil deeds.

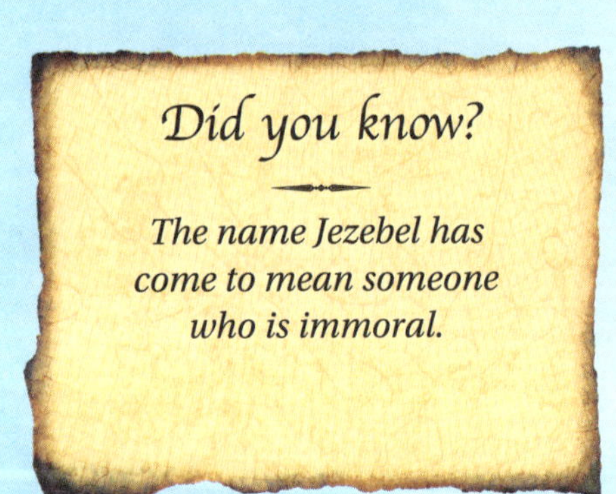

Did you know?

The name Jezebel has come to mean someone who is immoral.

Elijah, the Messenger of God

1 Kings 17:6 And the ravens brought him bread and meat in the morning, and bread and meat in the evening; and he drank from the brook.

One day, Elijah – the last of God's prophets left alive – visited Ahab and Jezebel.

"I've heard how you have tried to kill everyone who will not worship your wife's god," Elijah said bravely. "But I still serve God, and I've come to tell you that there will be no more rain until God allows it!"

The king and queen looked angry as Elijah walked away. "How dare he come and speak to us like that?" they said to each other. "We must have him killed!"

But after Elijah had delivered the message, God told him to go into hiding on the other side of the Jordan River.

In such a hot, dry country, rain was precious. When none fell, the crops withered and animals died. Food became scarce.

Elijah remained hidden where God had sent him, drinking from a stream and eating food that was dropped into his lap each day by huge black ravens. But soon the stream dried up.

"Now go to Zarephath where a widow will feed you," God told Elijah. So he made his way north and met a woman gathering sticks outside the city walls.

"Please could you fetch me a drink of water?" Elijah asked the woman. As she went to get the water, Elijah added, "and a piece of bread?"

The woman stopped. She was as poorly dressed as Elijah, and he could see that it was a long time since she had eaten anything.

"I'm sorry, but I don't have any food in my house. All I have is a handful of flour and a drop of oil," said the woman. "I'm gathering sticks so that I can make a fire and bake a pancake for my little boy. That's the last of our food."

"Don't worry," said Elijah. "Go make your pancake, but please make me a small cake first. God will look after you, and your son will always have flour in your barrel and oil in your jar."

The woman hurried home. Soon she rushed back to Elijah. "Here's your cake!" she cried, "and it's true! My barrel is full of flour, and my oil jar is full, too. You are truly a man of God. Please come and stay in our house."

Did you know?

At this time, the kingdom was divided into two: Israel in the north and Judah in the south.

Elijah and the Prophets of Baal

1 Kings 18:18 "I'm not the troublemaker," Elijah answered. "You are – you and your father. You are disobeying the Lord's commands and praising the idols of Baal."

Three years after Elijah's prophecy, God told Elijah to go and see King Ahab.

"Why have you come back, troublemaker?" asked Ahab, annoyed to see the prophet again.

"Send your people and the priests of Baal to meet me on Mount Carmel," replied Elijah. "We will have a contest to see who is the real God."

Everyone gathered on Mount Carmel, where Elijah said to the priests of Baal, "Build an altar to Baal. Put wood on it and place a sacrifice to Baal on top, but don't set it on fire. Call on Baal to send fire himself, to burn his sacrifice and then to end the drought for you."

Since Baal was supposed to be the god of rain and storms, people believed he would be able to send lightning to set the sacrifice on fire. The priests of Baal lifted up their arms and called, "Oh Baal, hear us!" But hours passed and the fire remained unlit.

"Perhaps he's asleep!" laughed Elijah. Then he gave orders for water to be poured over God's altar, so that the wood was too wet to burn. Then Elijah prayed to God, "Lord, prove now that you really are the God of Israel."

Suddenly, God sent down fire from Heaven - the pile of sodden logs burst into flames. Everyone fell down and praised God.

Almost immediately, the sky grew black and rain fell, ending the drought that God had sent to punish the people who had turned away from Him.

Elijah's Final Journey

2 Kings 2:12 Elisha saw it and cried out to Elijah, "My father, my father! Mighty defender of Israel! You are gone!" And he never saw Elijah again.

One day, Elijah was walking with his friend, Elisha. Elijah, knowing that he was going to die soon, asked Elisha not to travel with him any farther. But Elisha protested, saying, "I'm not leaving you!" So the two men continued walking on their way.

Elijah and Elisha reached a town named Bethel, and Elijah turned again to Elisha. "Stay here while I go on alone," he said. But Elisha wouldn't leave him.

Finally, they reached the Jordan River, and Elijah took off his cloak. He waved it toward the water, and the water split in two, leaving a path through the middle. Both men walked through. Then Elijah asked Elisha, "Is there anything you want to ask of me?"

"I would like to inherit your greatness and power, as if I were your son," Elisha replied.

"That might be difficult," said Elijah. "But if you see me while I am leaving this world, you shall have your request."

Suddenly, Elisha saw a chariot of fire appear out of the sky, pulled by horses of fire. Before he knew what was happening, Elijah was whirled up into the chariot and disappeared from sight. Elisha called after him, weeping, but Elijah was gone.

Sadly, he picked up Elijah's cloak and waved it toward the river. The waters parted and he walked through, realizing that he had inherited Elijah's powers.

The Story of Joash

2 Kings 12:2 Throughout his life, he did what pleased the Lord because Jehoiada the priest instructed him.

When Jezebel's grandson, King Ahaziah of Judah, was murdered, his mother, Athaliah, gave orders for the rest of the royal family to be murdered so that she could have the throne all to herself.

But Athaliah didn't notice that Joash, Ahaziah's baby son and Athaliah's grandson, had been snatched away by his aunt, Jehosheba. She hid him in a place where Athaliah would never look.

Jehosheba was married to the priest Jehoiada, and they cared for the baby secretly for six years. Then they decided that it was time to crown him king.

Jehoiada sent for the palace guards and swore them to secrecy. Everyone wanted to help make Joash king, since they hated Athaliah who did not worship the true God.

On the Sabbath day, when the Temple was full, the guards escorted Joash to the front.

"This is Joash, your king!" announced Jehoiada, and he anointed Joash and placed a crown on his head. The crowd clapped and cheered, "Long live the king!"

Athaliah heard the noise and hurried to the temple. She looked at the small boy and realized what had happened. "Treason!" she shouted. But the guards seized her instead, and her wicked reign was over.

Hezekiah Turns to God

2 Kings 18:13 In the fourteenth year of the reign of King Hezekiah, Sennacherib, the emperor of Assyria, attacked the fortified cities of Judah and conquered them.

Leading his army, Shalmaneser, the king of Assyria, destroyed homes and farms and murdered people as he marched through the kingdom of Israel.

In recent years, the people of Israel had disobeyed God and had returned to praying to false gods. Now their country was threatened – and many of them had been forced into slavery.

During this time, a wise and good man named Hezekiah was king of Judah. He destroyed the altars people had built to worship false gods and insisted that the Ten Commandments were kept. Then the Assyrians, under their new king Sennacherib, invaded the land of Judah.

Hezekiah sent Sennacherib a message to say that he would pay any price if the Assyrians would agree to leave his land. Sennacherib demanded so much silver and gold that even the Temple walls had to be stripped.

But although Sennacherib kept the treasure, he broke his promise and ordered his soldiers to attack Jerusalem. As they surrounded Jerusalem, Hezekiah went to the Temple to pray and ask the prophet Isaiah for help.

"Don't be afraid," answered Isaiah. "God will defend you."

That night, the Assyrian soldiers, waiting to attack beyond the city wall, went to sleep and never woke up again. When Sennacherib awoke and saw this, he realized he was up against a power much greater than himself. Terrified, he quickly returned home.

Amos and Hosea

Amos 9:11 The Lord says, "A day is coming when I will restore the kingdom of David, which is like a house fallen into ruins. I will repair its walls and restore it."

Amos was a sheep farmer who lived in the southern kingdom of Judah before the Assyrian invasions. God told him to go to Israel, so he took some wool to sell and journeyed north.

When he reached Bethel, Amos stood up in the marketplace and, as God had told him to, cried out, "You are cheating your customers! You use false weights so they get less than they pay for. Your prices are too high, and you sell poor people cheap rubbish - not the good grain that you have on show. If people can't pay you, you take the cloaks off their backs. God will not tolerate this!"

Amos noticed a wealthy woman wearing expensive clothes and perfume walking between the market stalls. He continued, "You women are to blame, too. You encourage your husbands to cheat, so that you have money to spend. Listen, you people of Israel! God says, 'be honest and show fairness and kindness to each other.'"

But the people did not listen. In fact, one of the priests threatened Amos, saying, "Go back to Judah and preach there." Amos left Israel but soon afterward, Hosea, a prophet from the northern kingdom, brought the same message.

Hosea was married to a pretty girl named Gomer. He loved her, but she didn't want to stay at home and look after their children. She wanted to go out and enjoy herself.

One day, Gomer went out and never came back.

Hosea was heartbroken. Then God spoke to him. "Hosea, I know how you feel. I love the people of Israel as much as you love Gomer, but they have gone away from me, just as Gomer left you. Do not stop loving Gomer, as I will not stop loving Israel. Go and find her, and win her back."

According to custom, Hosea was expected to divorce Gomer for her infidelity, but Hosea did as God said. Leaving someone to look after the children, he went to look for Gomer. She wasn't having fun as she had expected - a man had bought her as a slave.

Hosea gave all his money to the man to buy Gomer back. Both Gomer and Hosea had learned something valuable. Hosea began preaching differently. "Friends," he began, "I have realized that God's love is as constant as our own. As I love my wife in spite of her sin, so does God love his people in spite of theirs."

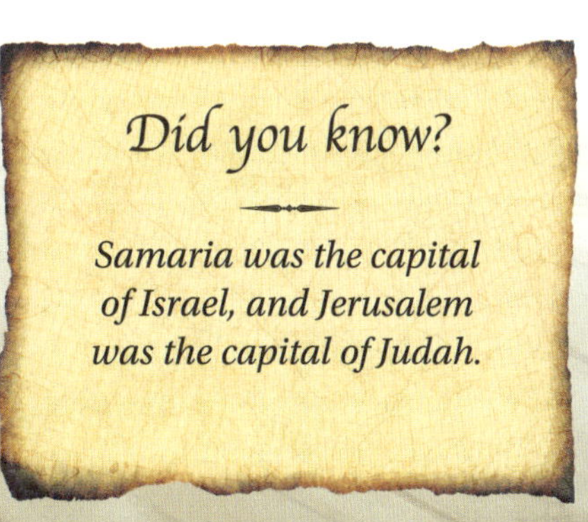

Did you know?

Samaria was the capital of Israel, and Jerusalem was the capital of Judah.

Jonah and the Storm

Jonah 4:2 "I know that you are a loving and merciful God, always patient, always kind, and always ready to change your mind and not punish."

One day, God told his prophet Jonah to go to the city of Nineveh, the capital of Assyria. The Assyrians were enemies of God's people. God said, "Tell the Assyrians that Nineveh will be destroyed in forty days unless they stop behaving wickedly!"

"I am not brave enough," thought Jonah. "I will not go - God will forgive them anyway!"

Jonah decided to go as far from Nineveh and God as he could, so he went to a place called Joppa and boarded a ship sailing to Spain.

As soon as the ship set sail, God whipped up a great storm. Waves crashed over the decks, and sailors fought to keep the ship upright. The captain went below deck and said to Jonah, "Pray to your God to save us!"

The sailors agreed that the cause of the storm had something to do with Jonah. They approached him, angrily.

"Yes," said Jonah. "I am the cause of the trouble. I am an Israelite, and I ran away from God. Throw me overboard - and the storm will stop."

The captain refused, but as the storm grew worse, he had no choice, and his men threw Jonah into the sea. The wind suddenly dropped and the water grew calm.

Jonah was sure that he would drown, and as he sank deeper into the ocean, he called out for help. God heard his cries, and in the next moment, Jonah found himself swallowed whole by an enormous fish.

For three days, Jonah sat inside the creature's huge, dark belly. He was truly sorry for disobeying God and apologized to Him in his prayers. God listened and made the fish swim to land and release Jonah.

"Go to Nineveh," God instructed Jonah for the second time.

The people of Nineveh listened to Jonah's message and immediately changed their ways. Everyone asked God for forgiveness, so he didn't destroy their city.

Jonah was cross. "I said you'd forgive them," he told God, as he marched out of Nineveh.

Jonah sat in the full glare of the sun, outside the walls of Nineveh. God made a vine grow to shade him. Then God made the vine wither and die. The sun beat down on Jonah once more.

"I'm sorry the plant has died. I was glad of it," said Jonah.

God replied, "Why do you care about a vine that you neither planted nor watered, while you begrudge my care for the happiness of a city of thousands of people?"

Suddenly, Jonah realized the true meaning of God's words.

Did you know?

Nineveh was an important city in ancient Assyria, now known as Iraq. It was in a central position between the Mediterranean Sea and the Indian Ocean.

Isaiah Foretells the Future

Isaiah 6:2 Around him, flaming creatures were standing, each of which had six wings.

Isaiah was one of God's prophets. Through him, God warned the people of Judah what would happen if they failed to obey His commandments. He also told them of the coming of the Messiah who would bring hope and freedom to everyone on earth.

One day, in the Temple in Jerusalem, Isaiah had a vision. He saw God sitting on His throne, high above everyone. God's robes were so vast that they twirled into every corner. Seraphs stood around Him, shielding their faces from His brightness with their fiery wings. Over and over again, they sang, "Holy, holy, holy is the Lord!" The sound of the seraphs' voices made the building tremble and smoke filled the air.

Isaiah was terrified. God was so great that he felt ashamed and cried out, "What will become of me? I belong to a wicked nation!"

At that moment, one of the seraphs flew toward Isaiah and touched his lips with a burning coal, saying, "Now your guilt is burned away – and you are without sin."

Then God asked, "Who will be my messenger?"

Isaiah replied, "I will!"

So God gave Isaiah his message but warned him that the people of Judah wouldn't listen or say they were sorry. But after what he had seen, Isaiah was determined to go and spread God's word.

Did you know?

Seraphs are a type of angel. They have six wings and are surrounded by dazzling flames of fire.

Ezra Shows the Way

Ezra 3:10 When the men started to lay the foundation of the Temple, the priests in their robes took their places with trumpets.

God had predicted that the people of Judah would not listen to Isaiah's message – and He was right. Trouble started to fall on them, and they were overthrown by enemies, leaving Jerusalem in ruins. Every time the people tried to rebuild it, their enemies destroyed it, and gradually everyone was forced to move away.

After several years, determined to make Jerusalem safe once more, some people returned to rebuild the Temple and city walls. Among them was a priest named Ezra. As soon as the Temple was secure, he read God's holy laws to the people of Judah who were gathered there.

"Praise the Lord, the great God!" Ezra exclaimed.

The crowd stood and shouted "Amen!"

Ezra reminded everyone of all that God had done for them and how they could please Him by not praying to false idols or turning their backs on Him. Soon they began to cry, "We haven't kept God's law properly."

Ezra reassured them. "God wants you to be happy! Go home and have a feast. Share your food and wine with anyone who does not have enough," he said.

The next day, everyone went back to hear more about God's laws from Ezra. They now all understood that He only wanted them to be honest and true.

Jeremiah and the Clay Pot

Jeremiah 19:10 "Then the Lord told me to break the jar in front of the men who had gone with me."

God told the prophet Jeremiah, "Go to the potter's workshop. I will give you a message there." So Jeremiah went to the workshop and watched as the potter shaped the clay and turned the pot on his wheel. Then the pot toppled and twisted. The potter stopped the wheel, pulled off the clay, and reshaped it. "It's important to get it right," he said.

"People are like clay," thought Jeremiah. "If things go wrong and they're sorry, God will make things better for them."

Next, Jeremiah bought a clay water pot and called the priests and leaders. He led them out of Jerusalem, the water pot on his head. A curious crowd followed him – men never carried water pots! When they arrived at the valley where people offered sacrifices to foreign gods, Jeremiah smashed the pot on the ground.

"Listen," he said, "God has waited for a long time for you to turn back to Him. He wanted to give you good things, but instead of being soft like clay, which the potter can shape, you have grown hard and defiant. If you don't turn back to God, you will be destroyed like that pot!"

Then Jeremiah climbed the steep path back into Jerusalem and preached the same sermon in the Temple.

Satan Tests Job

Job 1:11 "But now, suppose you take away everything he has – he will curse you to your face!"

Job was extremely rich. He owned hundreds of animals, had several children, and everyone liked him. He often prayed to God. But Satan, who hated God, said, "Job only worships you because he is wealthy. If things went wrong, he would blame you."

"Not true," said God. "Job loves me. Test him. Take away everything he owns. You'll see!"

Soon after, all of Job's animals were stolen. Next, a storm killed his children. Job thought, "Well, God knows best."

"Job has passed your test," God told Satan.

"Only because I haven't harmed Job himself," replied Satan.

"Then make him ill, but don't kill him," said God.

Suddenly, Job was covered in painful boils.

"God has done this to you!" complained Job's wife.

"Shh!" said Job. "You're happy when God gives us good things, we must accept it when he sends trouble."

Job's friends were shocked at his appearance. "What have you done?" they asked. "God must be punishing you for something."

"I've done nothing wrong," protested Job. "But you're right. Why is God being unfair to me?"

Then God spoke. He reminded Job that He was more powerful than Job could ever imagine. Job was ashamed. He realized he couldn't hope to understand everything God did. "I realize now that I'm not that important," he said.

Then God made Job better. He also restored his wealth and even gave him more children.

Did you know?

Satan is God's enemy, the one who challenges Him. He is sometimes said to be an angel who rebelled against God.

Daniel and His Friends

Daniel 1:15 When the time was up, they looked healthier and stronger than all those who had been eating the royal food.

During the fighting between Jerusalem and Babylon, many Jewish people were taken captive by the King of Babylon, Nebuchadnezzar. When they arrived in Babylon, Nebuchadnezzar ordered that several young and clever prisoners serve him at his court.

A handsome young man named Daniel and three of his friends, Shadrach, Meshach, and Abednego, were chosen.

The four men were clever and quick to learn, but Daniel had a special gift – he could interpret dreams. Although Daniel and his friends learned the Babylonian language and their way of life, he told an official, "We can't eat Babylonian food. Our God has given us rules about what we can and cannot eat."

The official was alarmed. "You must eat our food," he said. "If you don't and you grow weak, the king will punish me."

"Give us only water and vegetables for ten days," said Daniel, "and see how we look after that."

The official agreed, and after ten days, the four men looked healthier than the others who had been eating the king's food.

"All right, you can stay on your diet!" said the official. So Daniel and his friends remained loyal to God and their own people.

The Fiery Furnace

Daniel 3:28 "Praise the God of Shadrach, Meshach, and Abednego! He sent his angel and rescued these men who serve and trust him."

As the years passed in Babylon, Daniel became wiser, impressing King Nebuchadnezzar. Nebuchadnezzar made Daniel his chief advisor in Babylon. He also gave important jobs to his friends Shadrach, Meshach, and Abednego.

Later, Nebuchadnezzar gave orders for a huge gold statue to be built, fifteen times taller than a man, and that everyone must worship it. He invited everybody to come to the opening ceremony.

People came from all over Babylon to see this wondrous statue. Then an official announced, "When the musicians play, bow down and worship the statue!" Everyone obeyed – everyone, that is, except Shadrach, Meshach, and Abednego.

"How dare you!" raged the king. "Do as I say, or I'll have you thrown into a fiery furnace!"

"We will not worship your statue," they said. "Our God could save us from fire, but whether He chooses to or not, we will be loyal to Him."

Nebuchadnezzar had the furnace made seven times hotter than usual, and the men were thrown into the flames. Suddenly, Nebuchadnezzar looked horrified. He could see four men in the furnace. As they stepped out, their skin, clothing, and hair were untouched. The fourth person – an angel – disappeared.

"God sent His angel to save you!" cried Nebuchadnezzar. "From now on, my people will only worship your god!"

The Writing on the Wall

Daniel 5:5 Suddenly a human hand appeared and began writing on the plaster wall of the palace where the light from the lamps was shining most brightly. And the king saw the hand as it was writing.

The years passed in Babylon, and King Nebuchadnezzar died. The new king, Belshazzar, gave a great feast. He ordered that everyone should drink to their own gods and goddesses from the gold and silver goblets that were taken from the Temple in Jerusalem.

Although they were worried about using holy goblets for this purpose, his servants brought the sacred Temple treasures to the feast and filled the precious cups with wine. The guests laughed and drank, shouting toasts to their gods.

Suddenly, King Belshazzar turned pale. He was so frightened that his knees began to shake. He pointed a trembling finger to a white wall behind them, where a flickering candle lamp shone. "Look!" he whispered.

The laughter and chatter stopped. For there, against the wall, a floating hand was writing. When it stopped, the hand disappeared, leaving the words "MENE, MENE, TEKEL, UPHARSIN."

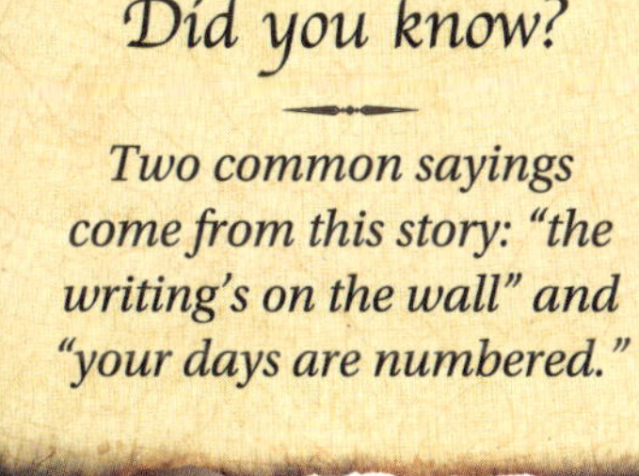

Did you know?

Two common sayings come from this story: "the writing's on the wall" and "your days are numbered."

"What do the words mean?" Belshazzar asked anxiously. But no one could tell him. "Anyone who can read the words and explain what it all means will be rewarded with riches beyond their dreams," the terrified king promised. But still, no one could translate the mysterious words.

Then Belshazzar's mother came to the room and said, "Call Daniel. God's spirit is in him, and he will know what the words mean."

So Daniel was called, and he looked carefully at the writing. Then he said, "I don't want your rewards, but I will explain the words to you. God has sent you a message. You have not learned about His greatness from the previous king of Babylon, King Nebuchadnezzar. Instead, you took the sacred cups from His Temple to use at your drunken party.

"MENE means 'number' – this means that the days of your reign are numbered. TEKEL means 'weight' – you have been weighed morally to see how honest you are and found to be unfair. UPHARSIN means 'division' – your kingdom will be divided between the Medes people and the Persians."

There was nothing that Belshazzar could do. That very night, enemy soldiers stormed the walls of the city. They killed Belshazzar and put their king, Darius of the Medes, on the throne in his place.

Daniel in the Lions' Den

Daniel 6:16 So the king gave orders for Daniel to be arrested, and he was thrown into the pit filled with lions. He said to Daniel, "May your God, whom you serve so loyally, rescue you."

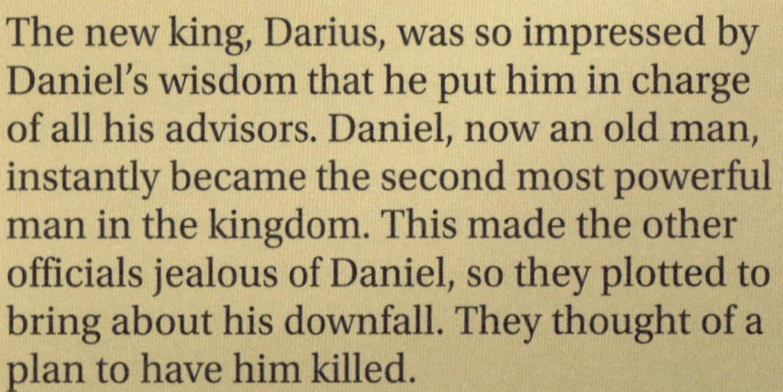

The new king, Darius, was so impressed by Daniel's wisdom that he put him in charge of all his advisors. Daniel, now an old man, instantly became the second most powerful man in the kingdom. This made the other officials jealous of Daniel, so they plotted to bring about his downfall. They thought of a plan to have him killed.

"Please sign this law," they said to Darius. The law declared that no one was to pray to any god except King Darius himself, for one whole month. Anyone who disobeyed this would be thrown into a pit where lions were kept. King Darius signed it.

Daniel heard about the law but continued to pray to God three times a

Did you know?

The Medes were an ancient race of people who lived in what is now northwestern Iran.

day, as he always had, in front of his open window, which pointed in the direction of Jerusalem. Daniel's enemies were delighted and watched him from the street. Their plan had worked. Triumphantly, they rushed off to tell the king.

What could Darius do? He had signed the law, so even though he loved Daniel, he could not find a way to save him. With a heavy heart, Darius gave the order for Daniel to be thrown into the lions' den. As soon as he was inside, the entrance was sealed. There was no escape.

"Only your God can save you now," called the king miserably, as he imagined the hungry lions eating his most trusted advisor.

That night, the king could not eat or sleep for thinking about Daniel. As soon as dawn broke, he hurried off to the lions' den.

"Daniel!" he called. "Has your God saved you?"

Darius didn't expect to find Daniel alive, so he was amazed to hear Daniel's voice reply, "The Lord sent His angel to stand beside me, and the lions have left me untouched. He did so because I am innocent and have done your Majesty no wrong."

The king was overjoyed and gave orders to have Daniel set free. Daniel walked out of the lions' den without even a scratch.

"Now everyone in my vast empire must respect your God, who does such wonderful things!" avowed Darius. Daniel stayed faithful to God for the rest of his life.

Ezekiel the Prophet

Ezekiel 1:28 It shone all over with a bright light that had in it all the hues of the rainbow. This was the dazzling light that showed the presence of the Lord.

Ezekiel was one of the young men that Nebuchadnezzar took from Jerusalem to serve him in Babylon.

Looking out of the palace window one night, Ezekiel saw four shining winged creatures in the sky pulling a dazzling figure in a gold and crystal chariot. Ezekiel guessed he was in God's presence.

"Ezekiel," said God. "Show my people in Babylon that more hardship is to come to Jerusalem."

Because God had prevented him from talking, Ezekiel carved a picture of Jerusalem with an army surrounding it onto a stone. A crowd watching him realized what Ezekiel was telling them. The next day, he made a tiny loaf and poured two cups of water. The crowd guessed that he was showing them that the people of Jerusalem would soon be going hungry.

The next day, Ezekiel cut off his hair and beard. He divided the hair into three piles, throwing one part on the fire, chopping another into pieces, and scattering the third to the wind. Then he carefully wrapped a few stray hairs in his cloak. Bystanders guessed that Ezekiel was showing what would happen to the people of Jerusalem. Some would die in a siege, others would be killed by swords, and the rest would be scattered far from home. God would take care of a few and give them a new beginning.

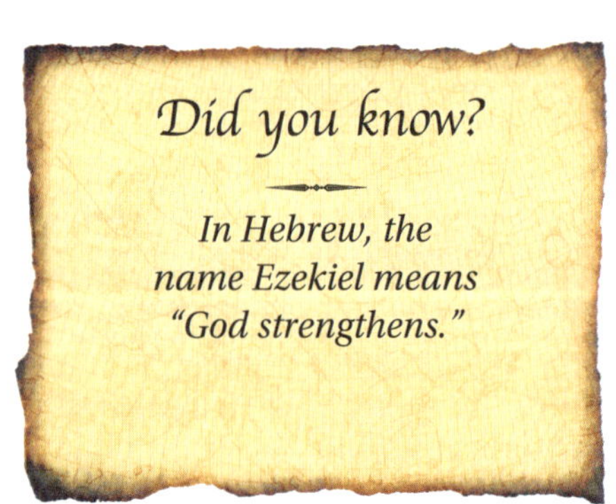

Did you know?

In Hebrew, the name Ezekiel means "God strengthens."

Nehemiah and the Wall of Jerusalem

Nehemiah 2:5 "If Your Majesty is pleased with me and is willing to grant my request, let me go to the land of Judah, to the city where my ancestors are buried, so that I can rebuild the city."

Nehemiah was one of the many Jews who lived in Babylon. He was the king's cupbearer. One day, Nehemiah's brother visited from Jerusalem. "Things are terrible," he told Nehemiah, sadly. "Jerusalem is still in ruins."

Later, when Nehemiah went to taste the king's wine, the king said. "You look sad, what's wrong?" Servants were not supposed to show their feelings, but Nehemiah answered boldly, "Jerusalem is still in ruins."

"Is there anything I can do?" asked the king.

Nehemiah made a quick, silent prayer to God. "I want to go back to Jerusalem to rebuild it," he said.

"Of course," said the king.

Nehemiah journeyed to Jerusalem and looked around. In some places, the city walls were reduced to rubble. The next day, he told everyone that God would help them to rebuild, and they all began working.

But the Samaritans - enemies of the Jews - watched and jeered, "Those Jews are pathetic - a fox could knock down those walls!"

So Nehemiah divided everyone into two groups. One group continued building, while the other group guarded them. Even those who were building carried weapons, and a man with a bugle was placed where he could see far away. If he spotted the enemy, he would sound the alarm.

The people were anxious. "God is with us," Nehemiah reminded them. "We won't be defeated now."

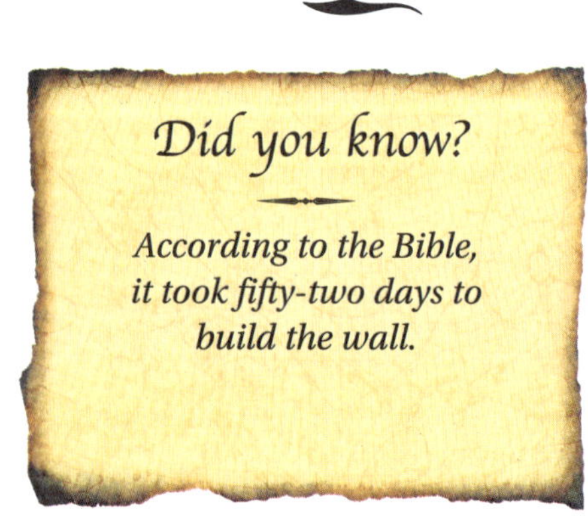

Queen Esther

Esther 2:17 The king liked her more than any of the other girls, and more than any of the others, she won his approval and affection.

Xerxes was now the ruler of the great Persian Empire that had conquered Babylon. He had many wives but wanted a new queen, so he ordered all the most beautiful girls to come to his luxurious palace.

Esther was a young, beautiful Jewish girl who, as an orphan, had been raised by her cousin Mordecai. Mordecai sent Esther to the Persian palace, saying, "Don't tell anyone you are Jewish."

The moment the king set eyes on Esther, he fell in love with her. "You shall be my queen!" he exclaimed, putting a golden crown on her head. The king held a great feast for Esther, and everyone stopped work to celebrate her arrival.

Later, Mordecai overheard two men plotting to kill the king. He told Esther, who told Xerxes at once, and the plot was foiled.

Xerxes then chose a new government official, Haman. Everyone bowed politely when Haman walked by, but Mordecai refused to bow.

"Why do you not bow to Haman?" the others asked him.

"I'm a Jew," he said. "And I only bow to God."

Haman was furious and vowed to punish all the Jewish people. He told the king that some people were troublemakers and should be killed. He issued an order that on the thirteenth day of the twelfth month, every Jew was to be murdered.

Did you know?

Because of Queen Esther, modern day Persian Jews are sometimes referred to as "Esther's Children."

Esther Saves the Jews

Esther 7:3-4 "If it pleases Your Majesty to grant my humble request, my wish is that I may live and that my people may live. My people and I have been sold for slaughter."

After the order to kill the Jews, Mordecai went to Esther. "Plead with your husband over this," he begged. So, for the sake of her people, Esther went to see Xerxes.

"What is it you want?" he asked.

"Will you and Haman dine with me tomorrow?" asked Esther.

That night, Xerxes couldn't sleep, so to pass the time, he read the palace records. When he read about Mordecai discovering the plot to kill him, he remembered that he had never rewarded Mordecai. The next day, he asked Haman, "How should I reward a man I wish to praise?"

Haman, believing that Xerxes meant him, said, "Dress him in royal robes, give him a crown, and proclaim him a hero."

"Yes, that's how I'll reward Mordecai!" said Xerxes, to Haman's dismay.

Later, Xerxes and Haman dined with Esther as she had asked.

Esther pleaded with the king, telling Xerxes for the first time that she was Jewish. "Please save me and my people – we're all about to be killed."

"Who would dare to kill you?" demanded Xerxes.

Esther pointed to Haman. "Him," she said. "He has already built the gallows to hang Mordecai."

"Then Haman will hang upon it!" said the king. "And Mordecai will become my new government official."

Introduction to the New Testament

The New Testament is a collection of writings that make up the second part of the Bible. The books of the New Testament contain both the teachings of Jesus and the early church's teachings about him. Jesus taught people how they should love God and how they should treat one another. He also taught that he was the Messiah who had been spoken about by the Jewish prophets whose writings are found in the Old Testament. The New Testament books teach us that Jesus is the Son of God, and that he died and came to life again to show God's love for humankind and to provide a way for our sins to be forgiven.

The New Testament consists of twenty-seven books, written in Greek by different people at different times, but all after Jesus' lifetime - probably between about AD 50 and AD 100. It can be divided into four parts: the Gospels, the Acts of the Apostles, the Epistles, and Revelations.

The four Gospels - written by Matthew, Mark, Luke, and John - tell the story of Jesus' birth, life, teaching, death, and resurrection.

The Gospels are followed by the Acts of the Apostles, also written by Luke. Acts is a sequel to Luke's Gospel, in which he tells how the early church was formed and how it grew, especially through the missionary work of the apostle Paul.

Next come some letters, often referred to as "Epistles." Some of these were written by Paul, some by other early church leaders such as Peter, James, and John. Some were written to individual people, others were written to particular churches, and some to the whole Christian church.

The last book in the Bible is known as Revelations, or the Revelations to John. This John was probably not the same John who wrote the Gospel or the epistles. In this book, he describes a series of visions he has had about how God will finally defeat evil once and for all, judge everyone according to what they have done during their lives, and establish a new Heaven and a new earth.

A Message from God

Luke 1:11-12 An angel of the Lord appeared to him, standing to the right of the altar where incense was burned. Zechariah was frightened.

Zechariah and Elizabeth were an elderly couple who lived during the time that Herod was the king of Judea. For many years, Elizabeth had tried to have a baby, but now she was too old.

Zechariah was a priest who worked at the temple. One day while he was busy working, he looked up and saw an angel next to the altar. The angel told him his name was Gabriel, and that he had come to tell Zechariah that his wife was at last going to have a baby. This baby was going to be very special. His name was to be John, and he was going to help the people who were living bad lives. They would become good again, in preparation for the coming of Jesus.

Zechariah was very surprised by this and told the angel Gabriel that he did not believe what he had told him. As punishment for his lack of faith, Gabriel told Zechariah that he would not be able to speak again until the baby was born.

Sure enough, Elizabeth became pregnant; nine months later, she gave birth to a baby boy. And Zechariah was not able to speak again until that time.

People expected the baby to be named Zechariah after his father, but much to everyone's surprise, Elizabeth and Zechariah insisted his name was to be John.

Did you know?

By naming their baby John, Zechariah and Elizabeth went against the tradition of naming the first son after the father.

An Angel from Heaven

Luke 1:45 How happy you are to believe that the Lord's message to you will come true!

When Elizabeth was about six months pregnant, God sent the angel Gabriel to Nazareth in Galilee. He went to tell Elizabeth's young relative, Mary, that she was also going to give birth to a baby boy. Mary was shocked and a little afraid, for she and Joseph were not yet married.

Gabriel reassured Mary, telling her not to be afraid. He said that her baby would be named Jesus and that he would be the son of God. Mary was still unsure, but Gabriel told her that the Holy Spirit would watch over her and keep her safe. The angel Gabriel reminded Mary that her cousin Elizabeth, who was too old to have a baby, was now nearly six months pregnant. He told her that God could make anything happen.

Mary decided to go to Judea and visit Elizabeth. When Mary arrived, Elizabeth was filled with the Holy Spirit, and her baby jumped for joy in her womb. She was moved and told Mary that she was blessed. Mary couldn't understand why God had chosen her to carry His son, but Elizabeth told her that God had blessed her because she had faith.

The Messiah Is Born

Luke 2:7 She gave birth to her first son, wrapped him in strips of cloth, and laid him in a manger – there was no room for them to stay at the inn.

Mary and Joseph were living in Nazareth in Galilee, where Joseph worked as a carpenter. One day, the Emperor Augustus decided that there should be a census. He wanted a list of the names of all the people who lived in his country, so he could tax them. Augustus ordered everyone to register in their own town.

Joseph's family came from Bethlehem, so he went there with Mary to register. The trip was long and difficult, especially for Mary because of the child she was carrying. So Mary rode on a donkey while Joseph walked beside her.

By the time Mary and Joseph finally arrived in Bethlehem, it was very busy. Unable to find anywhere to sleep for the night, Joseph walked from inn to inn asking for a room, but all the inns in Bethlehem were full.

At last, a kind innkeeper felt sorry for the couple. Seeing that Mary was heavily pregnant, he told them they could sleep in his stable for the night with the animals. Thanking the innkeeper, Joseph took Mary and the donkey to the stable. But they had hardly settled in for the night when Mary realized it was time for her baby to be born.

When the baby Jesus was born, there was no bed to put him in. So Mary wrapped the child in strips of cloth and laid him in a manger. As Jesus slept, the curious sheep, cows, and goats looked on from behind a haystack.

Not too far away, just outside Bethlehem, some shepherds were busy tending their sheep in the fields. Suddenly, an angel appeared before them in a flash of light. The angel told the shepherds not to be afraid and that he brought good news. He told them that their Messiah had been born, and they could go and see for themselves.

Then, as the shepherds listened, there was another flash of light, and the sky was filled with angels singing songs of praise to God. When the angels left, the shepherds decided it was time to go and see the baby for themselves.

The shepherds hurried to the stable and told Mary and Joseph what the angel had said about Jesus being the Messiah.

Did you know?

A manger is a long, narrow container into which farmers put food for their cows and horses.

The Three Wise Men

Matthew 2:2 "Where is the child who is born King of the Jews? We saw his star in the east and have come to worship him."

At the time when Jesus was born, Herod was the king in Judea. After Jesus' birth, some wise men were studying the stars and noticed a new star in the east. They believed that this star indicated the birth of the prophesied king, and that they should follow it and worship him.

After loading their camels, the wise men set off. But on their way to Bethlehem, the wise men lost sight of the star and stopped in Jerusalem to ask if anyone knew where they might find this new king of the Jews because they wanted to go and worship him. When King Herod heard of this, he was furious. The Romans had made Herod king of the Jews, and he didn't want a rival king in his land! Herod sent for the priests and teachers of God's law and asked them, "When the Messiah comes, where will he be born?"

On discovering that the baby would be born in Bethlehem, Herod thought of a plan. He sent for the wise men to find out when they had first seen the star.

"Go and look for the child in Bethlehem," Herod told the wise men. "When you find him, let me know, so that I can come and pray to him, too."

Believing what King Herod told them, the wise men set off in search of the child. Looking up at the night sky, they saw the star again moving slowly across the sky, and they knew that it would lead them to the baby Jesus. At last, the star stopped just over the place where Jesus was sleeping.

When the wise men saw the baby Jesus in Mary's arms, they fell to their knees and began to worship him. Then they opened their bags and took out treasures to offer to the new king. The wise men gave gifts fit for a king - of gold, frankincense, and myrrh.

That night, while the wise men were sleeping, an angel of God came to them and told them that Herod had devised an evil plan. The angel warned them that they should not tell him where the baby Jesus was. So early the next morning, the wise men set off for home, but instead of going back through Jerusalem, they followed the angel's advice and took a different route.

Did you know?

The Bible doesn't actually say there were three wise men, it just says "wise men." We assume there were three because they gave three gifts: gold, frankincense, and myrrh.

Herod's Order

Matthew 2:14 During the night, Joseph took the young child and his mother and escaped to Egypt.

Not long after the wise men had set off for home again, the angel of the Lord appeared to Joseph in a dream. He told Joseph to take Mary and Jesus to Egypt, far away from Bethlehem.

"King Herod plans to harm your baby, so you must leave quickly," the angel told Joseph. "You must stay in Egypt until I appear again to tell you to return to Israel."

Meanwhile, Herod was furious when he realized that the wise men had tricked him and that they had no intention of coming back. A cruel and evil man who had many enemies, Herod was always afraid that someone would kill him and seize his throne. So, to make sure that this baby king did not grow up, he ordered his soldiers to go to Bethlehem and kill every baby boy under the age of two years old.

The soldiers did as Herod ordered, taking the little boys from the arms of their mothers and killing them, just because Herod was afraid of losing his kingdom. Fortunately, Herod did not know that Jesus had already been taken far away from Bethlehem, where he was now safe.

The people of Bethlehem could never forget that terrible day, and they hated Herod more than ever.

Not long after this cruel event, King Herod died. As before, the angel of the Lord came to Joseph and told him that it was safe for him to take Mary and Jesus back to Bethlehem. But when they arrived in Israel, Joseph was dismayed to learn that Herod's son, Archelaus, was now the king. Instead of returning back to Bethlehem, Joseph took his family back to Nazareth, where he and Mary used to live and where he thought Jesus would not come to any harm.

As the years passed, Jesus grew up in Nazareth, and everyone who knew him loved him. This is why Jesus is sometimes called Jesus of Nazareth.

Did you know?
Herod had ten wives. His many families constantly fought each other in an attempt to gain power.

John Baptizes Jesus

Matthew 3:16 As soon as Jesus was baptized, he came up out of the water. Then Heaven was opened to him, and he saw the Spirit of God coming down like a dove and landing on him.

John the Baptist was very unhappy about the way people were living their lives, since they were not following God's rules. People were often unkind to each other and behaved sinfully. Deciding it was time to change things, John went to the banks of the Jordan River, since he knew that this was a place where people gathered to tell stories and exchange news while they did their washing and collected water.

John began telling all the people who gathered at the river about how they should live their lives according to God. He told them that they had to confess their sins and listen to how they could become good people.

"Soon, God will be coming to judge you all, and if you do not ask for forgiveness for your evil ways and wash yourselves in the Jordan River, you will not be allowed into Heaven," John preached.

One day while John was at the Jordan River, Jesus came from Galilee and asked John to baptize him in the river.

"Why are you coming to me for baptism?" John asked Jesus. "You are the one who should be baptizing me."

John felt that he was not important enough to accept this incredible privilege, yet Jesus insisted.

"This is how it must be for now," he told John. "I must show that I follow God in everything I do, and I must set an example for people to encourage them to confess their sins and be baptized, too." So John took Jesus into the river and

poured water over his head. As Jesus' head rose up out of the water, golden rays of light suddenly shone down from the sky. A white dove soared and swooped through the air and rested upon Jesus' head. The dove was the Spirit of God, and God said to Jesus, "You are my son, the one I love, and I am very pleased with what you have done."

Did you know?

People are baptized when they accept Jesus and join the Christian church.

Jesus Meets Satan

Luke 4:12 Jesus answered him, saying, "Scripture says, you must not test the Lord your God."

After he had been baptized by John, Jesus went into the desert by himself. For forty days and forty nights, Jesus ate nothing at all, fasting and praying and offering himself to God.

At the end of this time, his body gripped with hunger, Jesus heard a treacherous voice whisper, "If you are really the Son of God, then turn this stone into a loaf of bread."

"No!" said Jesus, knowing that the voice belonged to God's enemy, Satan, the Devil, who was trying to tempt him to use his great powers selfishly.

When this did not work, Satan showed Jesus all the great kingdoms of the world, the most powerful emperors, and the mightiest armies. "All this can be yours, if only you will bow down before me," he said. Once again, Jesus turned away.

But Satan had one more trick. He returned yet again as Jesus lay alone in the heat, feeling hungry and exhausted. This time, the Devil swept Jesus up to the highest part of the Temple in Jerusalem and said, "Go and throw yourself to the ground. If you really are the Son of God, then he will send angels to save you." Again, Jesus refused.

At last, Satan grew tired of trying to tempt Jesus into testing God and finally went away.

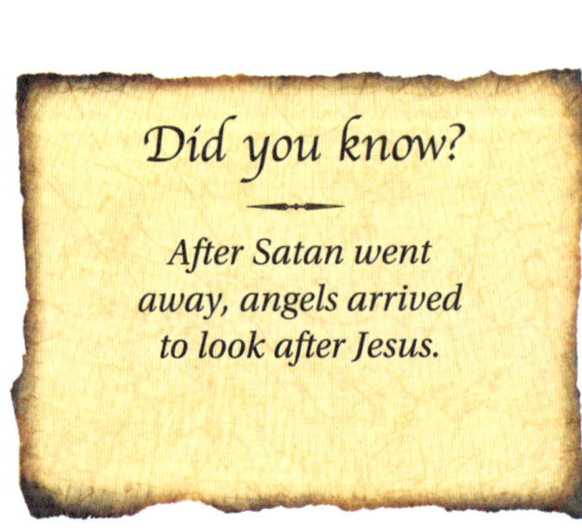

The Wedding at Cana

John 2:3 When the wine ran out, Jesus' mother said to him, "They have no wine."

One day, Jesus, his mother Mary, and some of their close friends were invited to a wedding feast in Cana, near Nazareth. Everyone was having a wonderful time, singing and dancing. But then Mary noticed that the wine had almost run out.

Mary went to Jesus and explained the problem. "If the guests are forced to drink water, it will bring disgrace to the bridegroom's father," she said.

Jesus said that there was nothing he could do, but Mary ignored his words and told the servants to do whatever Jesus instructed them to do.

Shortly afterward, Jesus told the servants to fill six huge earthenware pots with water. They sensed that Jesus was about to do something special, so they quickly obeyed.

"Now draw some of the water from a pot and take it to the master of the feast," said Jesus.

The puzzled servants watched while the master of the feast drank some of the liquid and announced, "This is the best wine I have ever tasted!"

The bridegroom was as confused as the servants. Where had this wine come from?

This was the first miracle that Jesus ever performed.

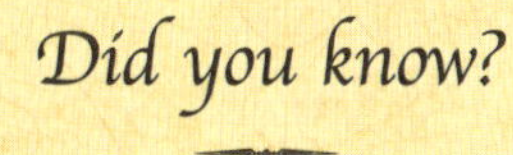

Did you know?

No one's sure of the exact location of Cana. The name means "place of reeds."

Jesus Meets the Fishermen

Luke 5:10 Jesus said to Simon, "Don't be afraid. From now on, you will be catching people alive."

Jesus was walking along the shore of the Sea of Galilee when he decided to stop and tell the people who were gathered there about the word of God. More and more people pushed their way into the crowd to hear what Jesus had to say. While Jesus was talking, he noticed two empty boats on the shore. The fishermen who owned them were busy washing their nets. Jesus asked the fisherman named Simon – who became known as Peter – to row him out from the shore. Simon obeyed, and Jesus continued his sermon to the crowdfrom the boat.

A little later, Jesus told Simon to push the boat out into the deep part of the lake and drop his fishing net. Simon knew that he and his friends had already tried to catch fish here, and there were none, but he had faith in Jesus, so did as he asked.

Simon and his friends, Andrew, James, and John, were amazed to see that they had caught so many fish that their net was heaving under the weight!

After filling two boats with the fish they had caught, Jesus told the four fishermen to leave their nets and follow him. They would now be catching people instead of fish. By this, Jesus meant that they would be preaching to people and getting them to follow the ways of God.

Jesus Heals the Sick

Mark 1:31 He came and took her by the hand, and helped her up. The fever left her, and she prepared a meal for them.

Simon became one of Jesus' closest friends. One evening, when Jesus visited his home, he was told that Simon's mother-in-law was very sick. She lay in bed, hardly able to breathe, and she was in great pain.

Jesus then took her hand and commanded the raging fever to leave her body. Simon's mother-in-law began to feel much better, so much so that she climbed out of bed. She had been cured!

Going downstairs, Simon's mother-in-law prepared a meal for everybody. The whole household was amazed to see how well she was, when she had been at death's door only moments before. She talked and laughed again as though she had never been sick.

Soon the news of Jesus' healing spread, and people began taking their sick friends and relatives to Jesus to heal. Jesus cured them all of their diseases and illnesses – he even drove the demons out of the minds of those who were troubled.

Jesus Heals the Leper

Mark 1:41 Jesus was filled with pity, and he stretched out his hand and touched him. "I want to help you," he answered. "Be healed!"

Jesus and his disciples were preaching around Galilee, teaching people about how they should follow God's rules and worship him. In one of the towns they visited, a man with leprosy, a terrible skin disease, approached Jesus and begged to be healed. Leprosy was a terrible curse, and people scattered in all directions when they saw the man. "He's unclean!" they cried.

Feeling sorry for the man, who had weeping sores all over his body, Jesus wanted to help him. He reached out and laid his hand upon the sick man. "Be healed," he said.

The man looked down at his once disfigured body and saw that he had been cured. His hands and feet were no longer deformed. The open sores covering his skin had also disappeared. He was well again!

Against Jesus' wishes, the leper could not resist telling everyone he met about how Jesus had healed him. Soon, all of Galilee knew of the miracle Jesus had performed, and sick people ran to him wherever he went.

The Paralyzed Man Walks

Matthew 9:6 Get up, pick up your mat, and go home.

By now, Jesus' teachings were spreading far and wide. He was teaching the people in Capernaum, a town on the Sea of Galilee, when hundreds of other men, women, and children crowded through the streets to listen to him speak.

Jesus was busy preaching inside his house when four men arrived carrying their paralyzed friend on a stretcher. They wanted Jesus to help their friend, but because there were so many other people, they couldn't get into his home.

The men had an idea. They hoisted their friend up onto the flat roof of the house. Then they cut a hole in the roof above the place where Jesus was standing. Once they had done this, they lowered the man down through the hole.

The owner of the house looked angry to see the paralyzed man being lowered through the hole, but Jesus smiled. He was moved by the strong faith the men had shown and told the paralyzed man his sins were forgiven.

The Pharisees and teachers of the law could not believe this. "Surely only God can forgive people's sins?" they asked Jesus.

"God has given me the authority to forgive people their sins," said Jesus. "And to prove this, I will heal this man."

Turning to the paralyzed man, he told him, "Stand up and walk!"

The man stood, thanked Jesus, and went home. "Praise God!" the people cried.

Did you know?

The Pharisees were Jews who followed Moses' laws very strictly. Jesus criticized them for being hypocrites. The apostle Paul was a Pharisee before becoming a Christian.

Jesus Calms the Storm

Luke 8:24 Jesus got up and gave an order to the wind and the stormy water; they died down, and there was a great calm.

After a long day of teaching parables, Jesus needed to rest. He asked his disciples to take him in a boat to the other side of the Sea of Galilee, where he could have some peace and quiet.

Feeling very tired, Jesus climbed into the disciples' boat, rolled up some cloth as a pillow, and quickly fell asleep.

The disciples, who weren't the least bit tired, sat talking to each other about that day's teachings.

Suddenly, without warning, a strong wind began to blow. It whipped the water into a frenzy, and the boat began rocking and shifting unsteadily.

When one of the disciples stood up to adjust the ropes, he was almost thrown into the water. Another huge gust of wind blew and brought a gigantic wave with it. As the boat rocked violently from side to side, it began to fill with water.

Did you know?

A parable is a simple story that is used to teach people lessons.

The disciples were brave men and had sailed in boats many times before, but this storm was more powerful than any they had ever seen.

Beginning to get worried, the men wondered how Jesus could sleep through such a storm. They shook him awake and cried, “Wake up! Wake up! We are all going to drown!”

Calmly, Jesus stood up in the boat, raised his hand to the fierce waves, and commanded them to be still. The disciples watched in amazement as the wind stopped howling, the waves stopped crashing, and everything became quiet and calm.

As they stared at him in wonder, Jesus looked at his disciples and asked them why they did not have faith. The disciples did not reply. Feeling a little afraid of Jesus, they wondered who this man, who looked like any other, could really be. They could hardly believe his power, but they chose to believe that he really was the Son of God.

Jairus' Daughter

Matthew 9:22 But Jesus, turning around and seeing her, said, "Daughter, cheer up! Your faith has made you well." And the woman was made well from that hour.

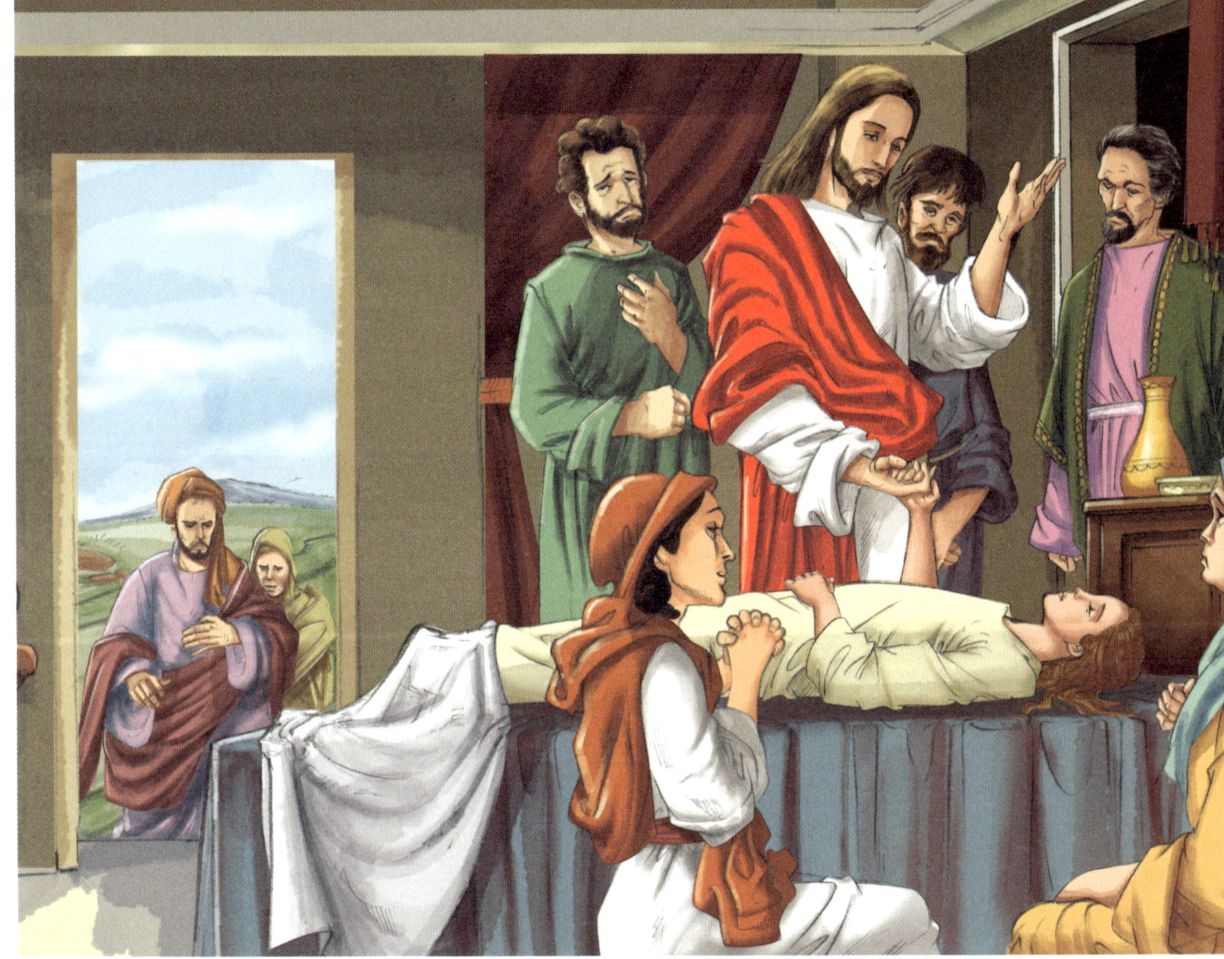

One day in Capernaum, a man named Jairus pushed his way through the crowd that had gathered around Jesus. Throwing himself down at Jesus' feet, he begged him for help.

Jairus explained that he was an official in the local synagogue whose young daughter was very sick. She was only twelve years old, his only daughter, and he loved her very much. In a voice desperate with emotion, Jairus asked Jesus to lay his hands on his beloved daughter and make her well.

Looking down at the solemn, well-dressed man who was kneeling in the dirt, Jesus said, "I will come to your house at once."

As he followed Jairus, a large crowd followed closely behind them. Jesus suddenly stopped, turned to the crowd, and asked, "Who touched my coat?"

At first, everyone denied it, but Jesus said, "I know someone touched my coat, and when they did I felt a power pass out of my body."

Finally, a woman came forward and knelt at Jesus' feet. In a shaky voice, she said, "I have been very ill for twelve years, but I thought that if I could only touch your clothing, then I might be healed."

Jesus smiled and told the woman that she had been healed. In disbelief, the woman saw that Jesus' words were true. Her pain had gone for the first time in many years, and she was completely well again!

As the woman walked away happily, some people ran toward Jairus to tell him that his daughter had died. Falling to his knees, Jairus began to weep.

"Have faith," Jesus told Jairus. "Your daughter is not dead; she is only sleeping."

Jesus sent the crowd away and continued on with Jairus to his house. The apostles Peter, James, and John went with them.

When they arrived at the house, Jesus told the gathering mourners to stop crying, since the girl was not dead. When the mourners looked at him in disbelief, Jesus sent them outside. Then he took Jairus, the girl's mother, and the three disciples into the girl's room.

Holding her hand, Jesus gently whispered, "Little girl, get up now." Jairus' daughter got out of bed and began walking around. She was alive!

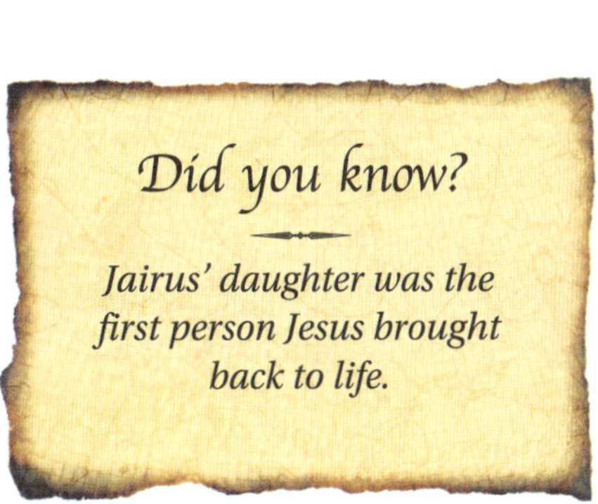

Did you know?

Jairus' daughter was the first person Jesus brought back to life.

Jesus Calls Matthew

Mark 2:17 Jesus heard them and answered, "People who are well do not need a doctor, only those who are sick."

Jesus was feeling tired as he walked along the shore of the Sea of Galilee. In the past few months, he had performed many miracles: healing sick people, turning water into wine, driving out evil spirits, and even raising people from the dead. Jesus had also journeyed a long way, teaching many people about how they should lead good lives.

As Jesus walked along the shore, a large crowd of people came up to him. They wanted him to talk to them and tell them about the word of God. They wanted him to teach them how to lead useful lives and be good people. So Jesus began telling them how wonderful God was and how they would be rewarded in Heaven if they had faith in God and followed his rules.

When Jesus had finished speaking, he continued on his way. Then something caught his eye. Jesus looked up and saw Matthew sitting at his desk in a large building. Matthew was a tax collector, so most people did not like him or want to talk to him. In fact, most people despised Matthew simply because he collected their taxes.

Matthew looked very sad and lonely when Jesus went to him and said, "Leave all your things and follow me." Without a second thought, Matthew left everything behind and followed Jesus. Matthew was so happy to finally have a new friend that he decided to hold a big feast. He invited Jesus and the disciples - and even some other tax collectors and lonely people. Matthew spent the whole day preparing for the meal.

During the feast, while everyone was busy eating, some Pharisees and law teachers came by and saw Jesus eating with the tax collectors and outcasts. They were outraged and asked the disciples why Jesus would want to spend time with people that nobody liked.

Overhearing the Pharisees' comments, Jesus told them that the outcasts were the people who most needed his help, and he would not turn his back on them. He would teach them the ways of God and make them better people.

Did you know?

People did not like tax collectors, since they could keep the extra money they collected from people for themselves.

The Disciples Are Chosen

Mark 3:14 He appointed twelve men to be with him, who he could also send out to preach.

As Jesus and his disciples were at the Sea of Galilee, a huge crowd began to gather. The people had come from all over the country to see Jesus. There were so many people pushing and trying to get close to him that Jesus was afraid for his safety. He asked his disciples to fetch a boat for him. Then, climbing into the boat, Jesus finished his sermon from there.

When the crowds had left, Jesus asked his twelve most trusted disciples to follow him up a steep hill so that he could speak to them privately. The disciples were the brothers James and John, Simon (whom he now called Peter), and Andrew, Philip, another James, Simon the Zealot, Thaddaeus, Bartholomew, Thomas, Matthew the tax collector, and Judas Iscariot. Judas was the disciple who eventually was to betray Jesus.

"I have chosen you to do something very important," Jesus said. "I am asking you to continue my mission to spread God's word." He told them that he had chosen them to help him teach people God's word by visiting towns and villages as he had done. After that, they were to travel far and wide in order to spread Jesus' teachings to all of God's people. In order to do this, he gave them the power to drive out evil demons from people and to heal the sick. He warned the disciples that they would face many obstacles, but that God would always give them the courage they needed.

The disciples were determined to do as Jesus suggested and began to spread his teachings. From that day on, the twelve disciples came to be known as the twelve apostles.

Did you know?
A disciple is anyone who follows Jesus. The word is most often used when talking about the twelve main disciples, or apostles.

The Death of John the Baptist

Matthew 14:9 And the king was sorry: Nevertheless, for the oath's sake, and for those who sat with him at the feast, he commanded that John be killed.

King Herod had arrested John the Baptist and thrown him into prison because he had criticized the king. John had told King Herod that he was wrong for divorcing his wife and then marrying his brother's wife, Herodias. Herodias was also Herod's niece, so John the Baptist told him that he had broken the law of Moses by marrying within his family.

On Herod's birthday, he held a big feast with lots of important guests and asked Herodias' daughter, Salome, to perform a dance. Herod was so impressed with her dancing that, in front of everyone, he told her that he would give her anything she wanted. Salome thought for a little while, then her mother whispered in her ear. Salome smiled and demanded the head of John the Baptist on a silver platter.

A shocked silence spread throughout the room. Herod had imprisoned John the Baptist as punishment but did not want to kill him. But he had made Salome a promise in front of all the guests, so he could not refuse her without losing respect.

Herod spoke to a soldier who returned a few moments later confirming that John the Baptist had been killed.

The Feeding of the Five Thousand

Luke 9:17 They ate until everyone was full. Then they gathered up twelve baskets of broken pieces that were left over.

Jesus and his disciples were talking to a crowd of people when they learned that John the Baptist had been killed by Herod. The busy Passover feast was to take place soon, so they decided to go somewhere quiet to rest and think.

Jesus and his disciples climbed into a boat and sailed across the Sea of Galilee to the northern shore. But when Jesus looked around him, he saw huge crowds walking or on donkeys, coming toward him along the coast. When they arrived, Jesus felt sorry for these all these people who wanted to be taught, so he began to teach them. Jesus talked until it was very late.

"You should send the people away now, Jesus," said the disciples. "They are hungry, and we have no food to give them." But Jesus knew what to do. He told the disciples to go and find what food they could.

The disciples found a young boy who had two fish and five loaves of bread, which was not nearly enough to feed the thousands of people who had gathered around Jesus.

But Jesus took the fish and the loaves and blessed them. And when they were given out to the crowd to eat, everyone got enough to satisfy their hunger. There were even twelve baskets of bread left over at the end!

Miracle at Sea

Matthew 14:31 "How little faith you have. Why did you have doubts?"

After Jesus had fed the people with loaves and fish, he needed to rest. Jesus told his disciples to take the boat and return to the other side of the Sea of Galilee without him. The disciples set off immediately, and Jesus began walking up a hill that looked quiet and secluded. Finally reaching the top, Jesus sat down and began to pray.

When he had finished praying, Jesus looked out over the Sea of Galilee and took in the beautiful scenery around him.

He could just make out the disciples in their little boat, in the middle of the sea.

Suddenly, the wind began to blow. The flowers and grass danced with the breeze. Then the wind blew stronger, and the trees bent under the force.

As the wind picked up speed, Jesus' cloak started to billow around him. He looked out again and tried to find the little boat, but the huge waves were hiding it from view. At last, Jesus saw the boat lurching violently in the rough sea.

Jesus wanted to make sure that his disciples were safe. He made his way toward the shore and began to walk on the water toward the disciples' boat.

When the disciples saw Jesus walking on the water, they were terrified and screamed in fear. They thought Jesus was a ghost.

"Don't be afraid. It is me," said a voice so gentle and familiar.

Not all the disciples were convinced and sat frozen in the boat. But Simon knew, beyond doubt, who the voice belonged to. "Lord," he said, "if it is really you, then tell me to come to you across the waves."

"Come to me," said Jesus, stretching out his hand. Simon slowly climbed out of the boat and stood up. He was standing on the water! Then he walked carefully over to where Jesus was waiting for him.

Suddenly, a gust of wind whipped at Simon's face, and he became afraid. Immediately he fell down into the water and began to sink into the freezing depths. "Save me, Lord!" he cried.

Jesus grabbed Simon's arm and pulled him up.

"O man of little faith, why did you doubt?" asked Jesus, holding Simon firmly by his shoulders. Then Jesus guided Simon back into the boat, and the wind ceased to blow.

Gazing at Jesus in wonder, his disciples exclaimed, "You are surely the Son of God!"

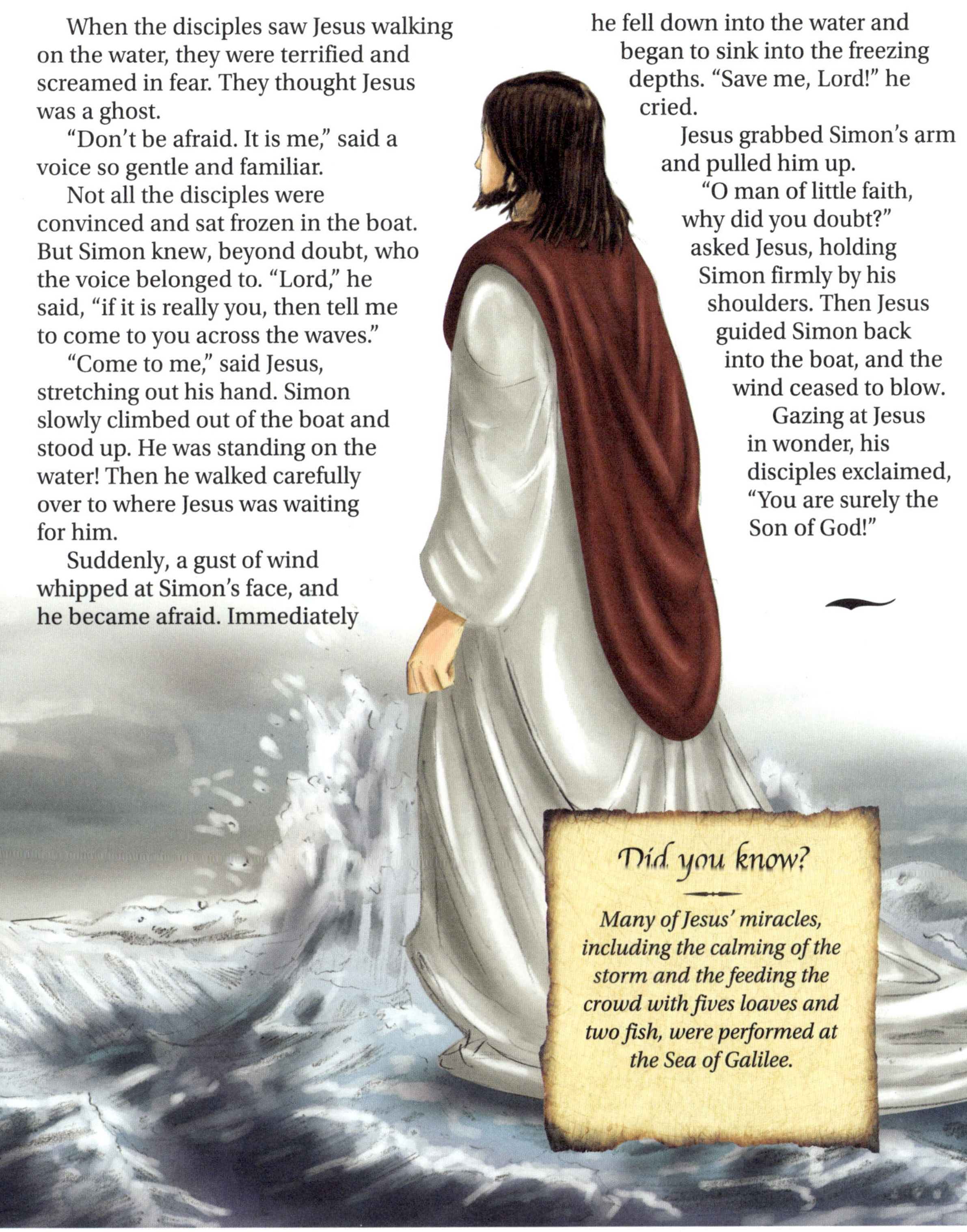

Did you know?

Many of Jesus' miracles, including the calming of the storm and the feeding the crowd with fives loaves and two fish, were performed at the Sea of Galilee.

The Sermon on the Mount

Matthew 5:5 Blessed are the gentle, for they shall inherit the earth.

Everywhere Jesus went, crowds of people seemed to follow him. They had heard how he could perform miracles, so they were curious to know more about him. People wanted to be healed; some had friends and relatives who they wanted Jesus to heal. But this wasn't the only reason people gathered when Jesus was nearby; they also wanted to be taught how to be good and live decent lives.

Jesus was out walking one day when a crowd gathered and asked him to speak. So he climbed up a hill and sat down. The people followed him and sat close by.

Jesus spoke first about happiness – what it was and how to find it. "You will only be truly happy when you are rewarded in Heaven for being gentle, unselfish, and pure – for trying to create a peaceful world to live in," Jesus told the crowd.

"God's creations are like salt," Jesus went on to tell the people. "But if salt loses its taste, there is no way to make it salty again. It has become worthless – and must be thrown out."

The crowds listened in silence as Jesus continued, "You are like a light for the whole world that cannot be hidden. No one lights a lamp and puts it under a bowl; instead, he puts it on the lamp stand, where it gives light to everyone. In the same way, your good deeds act as a light for other people. When you lead good lives, others will see the good things you do and will praise your Father in Heaven."

Jesus went on to talk about the laws of the Ten Commandments and how they must be followed in order for people to be welcomed into Heaven. He told people that they should control their tempers and make peace with their enemies – because, when the time came for them to be judged, God would judge them for any anger they had felt toward others.

"You must love your enemies and give charitably. You must help those who live nearby and friends who need it," said Jesus. "Forget about earthly riches, such as money and gold. Instead, store up riches in Heaven by doing good deeds on earth."

This sermon that Jesus taught on the mountainside became known as the Sermon on the Mount.

Did you know?

Jesus' Sermon on the Mount includes many lessons that we say today; for example, "turn the other cheek," meaning to walk away from someone who makes you angry.

The Lord's Prayer

Matthew 6:5 "When you pray, you are not like the hypocrites, who love to stand and pray in the synagogues and in the corners of the streets, so that people will see them."

One day, when the disciples were alone with Jesus, they asked him how they should pray. "You should pray simply," Jesus told his followers. "You do not need to pray for hours where everyone can see you and say what a good person you are. Instead, go somewhere private and close the door so that nobody will see you."

That day, Jesus explained to his disciples and followers that when they prayed, they should think about the words that they were saying and what they really

meant. It did not matter if the prayers were long or short, only that they were thinking hard about what they meant.

Jesus then gave the disciples a prayer, now known as the Lord's Prayer, that they could say when they were praying:

Our Father, who art in Heaven,
hallowed be thy name.
Thy Kingdom come,
thy will be done,
on earth as it is in Heaven.
Give us this day our daily bread.
And forgive us our trespasses,
as we forgive those who trespass against us.
And lead us not into temptation,
but deliver us from evil.
For thine is the kingdom, the power,
and the glory, forever and ever.
Amen.

When the disciples had all prayed together for a while, Jesus told them that they must always pray to God and encourage others to pray, too. "Never give up," he said.

Jesus then gave the disciples an example of what he meant. "Imagine you knock on the door next door in the middle of the night because you urgently need to borrow something from them," said Jesus. "After being woken from a night's sleep, most people would be angry and simply ignore your knocking and calling before going back to sleep. But if you are persistent and keep calling to them, the person will find it hard to ignore you. If for no other reason than to make you be quiet, he will open the door and give you what you want; not because he is being a good friend, but because you are making so much noise!"

Jesus' disciples laughed at his story, but they understood the meaning. They would never give up praying or preaching God's word, despite the fact that some people would be more willing to listen than others.

Did you know?

The last line of the Lord's Prayer – For thine is the kingdom, the power, and the glory, forever and ever – is not used by Roman Catholic Christians.

Jesus and the Accused Woman

John 8:7 "He among you who is without sin, let him throw the first stone at her."

Jesus had spent the night up on the Mount of Olives, quietly thinking and praying. Early the next morning, as he made his way back, Jesus decided to stop by the temple. A crowd soon gathered when they saw Jesus, and people asked him to tell them more about God.

While Jesus was talking, some scribes and Pharisees came into the temple, pulling a very frightened woman along after them. They pushed the woman in front of Jesus and told him that she had been unfaithful to her husband. One of the Ten Commandments orders that people should not commit adultery, so this was very serious - and the punishment was death by stoning!

"This woman should be stoned at once!" said the scribes and the Pharisees, who were testing Jesus because they knew that he wouldn't want the woman to be harmed. But if he said no, then Jesus would be going against the laws of the Old Testament.

Jesus thought for a moment, then said, "All right, stone her. Whichever one of you has never sinned can throw the first stone."

Suddenly, there was complete silence in the temple, then one by one, the scribes and Pharisees left, until only Jesus and the woman remained.

Not one of the accusers could say that they had never sinned, so they were all as guilty as the accused woman.

Jesus Foresees His Death

Matthew 16:24 Then Jesus said to his disciples, "If anyone wants to be my follower, he must not think about himself, take up his cross, and come with me."

Jesus knew that he was going to be killed. There were many people, including King Herod, who did not agree with his teachings or the way that he criticized the bad lives they were living.

Jesus even had a vision of how he would be killed. His enemies were going to hang him on a cross.

Jesus decided that it would be best to tell his disciples that he would be leaving them soon. "I won't leave you on your own," he said. "God will send His spirit to be with you. Don't worry - and don't be afraid."

Jesus went on to tell his disciples that the priests, the law teachers, and other officials were against him and were going to kill him.

"But you could prevent your death if you wanted to!" said Peter.

But Jesus explained that it must be this way. "Everyone who follows my example, and those that have lived their lives for God, will meet me again and be rewarded in Heaven," he told Peter and the other disciples.

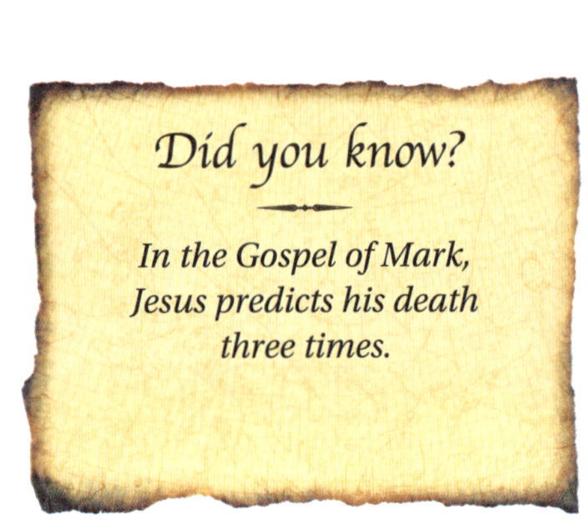

Did you know?

In the Gospel of Mark, Jesus predicts his death three times.

The Transfiguration

Mark 9:7 A cloud cast a shadow over them, and a voice came out of the cloud, "This is my beloved son. Listen to him."

A few days after Jesus had told his disciples of how he would be killed, he took three of them – Peter, John, and James – with him to the top of a high mountain.

Leaving his disciples, Jesus went off to find a quiet spot to pray. Suddenly, something amazing happened – he was changed, or transfigured. His face began to shine like the sun – and his clothes became as white as the purest snow. As Jesus stood there, two figures appeared at his side.

"Who are those people?" asked the disciples, shielding their eyes.

The disciples shook their heads. The two men looked like prophets from long ago. At last, Peter realized who the men were: Moses, who had led the Israelites to the Promised Land, and Elijah, the greatest of all the prophets! They were speaking to Jesus about his death, which was going to take place in Jerusalem.

"Your death and resurrection will set people free," said Moses, as the disciples, looking a little afraid, listened.

"Lord, it's lucky for us to be here with you," said Peter. "We will make three tents – one each for you, Moses, and Elijah – and then ..." Poor Peter was so shocked at seeing Moses and Elijah standing before him that he didn't really know what he was saying.

Then, suddenly, a cloud appeared over them. Again the disciples were gripped with fear as a voice said, "This is my son, the chosen one. You must listen to him!"

The voice stopped, and the cloud disappeared. The disciples knew they had heard the voice of God speaking to them, and they fell to their knees, casting their eyes to the ground. When they looked up again, Jesus was alone – and the brightness had gone.

Jesus asked his disciples not to tell anyone about what they had seen that day on the mountain until after he had died and been resurrected.

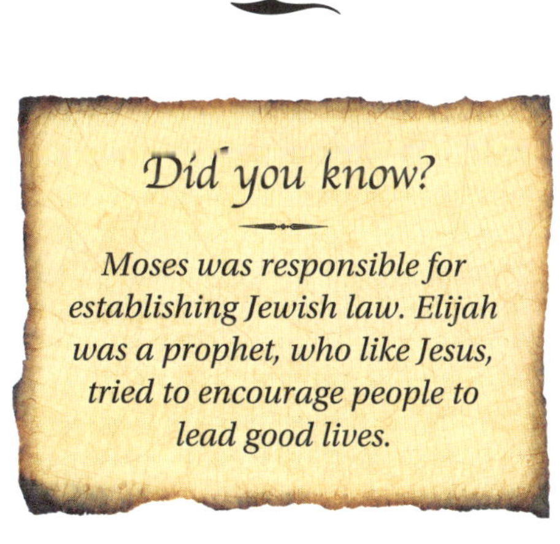

The Good Samaritan

Luke 10:27 Love the Lord your God with all your heart.

One day, one of the Pharisees asked Jesus a difficult question, in an attempt to catch him out. He asked, "What must I do on Earth to make sure that I go to Heaven when I die?"

Jesus replied, "What does God's law tell us about that?"

The man answered, "That we must love God with all our hearts and love our fellow man as much as we love ourselves."

"Yes," said Jesus. "Do this and you will live forever in Heaven."

But the man was not satisfied. "So what exactly does God want me to do?" he asked. Jesus told a story to explain.

"One day, a man was journeying from Jerusalem to Jericho. Nobody liked using this road because there were many large boulders that thieves could hide behind. Suddenly, some thieves sprang from their hiding place and attacked the vulnerable man. The robbers beat him, stole his clothes and money, and ran away, leaving him badly hurt.

"After a while, a priest passed by. He saw the man lying there but crossed to the other side of the road and quickly walked on.

"Soon after, a Temple worker came along. He looked at the naked, wounded man but then hurried on his way.

"Some time later, a Samaritan riding a donkey saw the man. Jews and Samaritans were enemies, but the Samaritan's heart filled with pity at the sight of the injured man. He got down from his donkey and began to clean up the man's wounds with cool wine and soothing oil. Then he bandaged his wounds, carefully lifted him onto his donkey, and led him to the nearest inn.

"When the Samaritan arrived, he gave the innkeeper two silver coins. 'Take care of this man,' he said, 'and when I come back this way, if it has cost you more to look after him, I will pay you.'"

When he had told his story, Jesus looked at the religious leader and said, "Which of the three passersby showed love to the injured man?"

"The one who looked after him," answered the man, who didn't like admitting it was the Samaritan – one of the Jews' enemies!

Jesus replied, "That's right. Now go and be like the good Samaritan."

Did you know?
Samaritans came from Samaria, to the north of Judea. Because of differences in customs and religion, there was a lot of bad feeling between them and the Jews.

The Lost Sheep

Luke 15:7 "… there will be more joy in Heaven over one sinner who repents than over ninety-nine righteous persons who do not need to repent."

Large crowds followed Jesus to listen to his teachings. The law teachers went too, but they were annoyed to see some people in the crowd who broke their laws.

One man commented, "Jesus welcomes these outcasts. I hear he even eats with them!"

"He can't be a teacher from God if he does that," remarked another man. "God wouldn't encourage sinners."

Jesus overheard this conversation and told the men a story.

A man owned a hundred sheep. One night, when he counted them, one sheep was missing. What could he do? Settle down for the night with ninety-nine sheep, or go and search for the lost one?

Of course, he went in search of the lost sheep. Even though he was weary, the man retraced his steps. At last, he heard a faint bleat – and there was his lost sheep!

When he arrived home, the man threw a party for all of his friends, wanting them to share his joy in finding his lost sheep.

"God feels about people the way the man felt about His sheep," Jesus told the men. "Even though some people may become lost and forget God's teachings, He will always help them to find the correct path again."

The Foolish Bridesmaids

Matthew 25:10 The five girls who were ready went in with him to the wedding feast, and the door was closed.

Jesus told a story about a wedding. Once, a bride and her ten friends were waiting for the groom to arrive. In case they had to wait a long time, five girls had brought extra oil for their lamps but the other five had not. Night came, and they all fell asleep.

Suddenly, at midnight, someone called, "The groom is on his way!"

The girls awoke and turned up their lamps. "Oh, no!" cried five of them. "We have run out of oil! Please lend us some!"

"Sorry, but we have none to spare," answered the five sensible girls. So the other five girls rushed off to buy more oil for their lamps.

While they were away, the groom arrived. The bride and the five sensible girls joined the wedding procession to his house. Some time later, the five foolish girls arrived at his house. "Let us in!" they called.

From inside, the groom replied, "No! I don't know who you are."

When Jesus finished the story, he told the disciples that one day, the Messiah would come back. No one knew when that would be, so they had to be ready, or they would be too late to follow him.

The Prodigal Son

Luke 15:18 "Father, I have sinned against God and against you. I am no longer fit to be called your son."

Jesus told a number of stories, or "parables," to explain God's love. One of these stories was about a farmer who had two sons.

One day, the younger son said to his father, "I'm tired of being at home and doing as I'm told. I want to go away, so please give me my share of the family fortune."

The father gave his son his share of the wealth, and the boy set off. He soon made new friends and had a great time, spending his money freely.

One morning, the boy awoke to find that all his money had gone – along with his new friends. Worse still, there was a severe famine in the land, so there was little work or food around.

Eventually, the boy found some work. His job was to look after pigs, which was hard and tiring. He worked long days for little money, and soon he was starving.

"I have been very stupid," he thought. "On my father's land, even the workers have good food to eat. If I go back and say sorry, I don't expect my father to forgive me, but he might give me a job on the farm."

He set off at once. When his father saw him, he couldn't believe his eyes. He ran toward his son and threw his arms around him.

"Fetch my best robe and sandals for my son," the farmer told his servants. "Put my ring on his finger, then kill the calf we've been fattening up. We're going to have a party!"

By the time the elder son returned home from working on the fields, the party had begun. "What's happening?" he asked the servants.

"Your brother has come home," the servants replied.

The elder brother was furious. "I've worked for you all these years," he told his father, "but you have never given a party for me. Then my brother, who has wasted all your money, comes home and you kill the prize calf to feed him."

The father looked upset. "But son," he said, "everything I own belongs to you. We are together all the time. But your brother was lost, and now he's been found. That is why we are celebrating today."

Did you know?

"Prodigal" means extravagant or wasteful. It describes the young son before he returns home.

Lazarus and the Rich Man

Luke 16:25-26 "But Abraham said, 'Remember, my son, that in your lifetime you were given all the good things, while Lazarus got all the bad things. But now he is enjoying himself here, while you are in pain.'"

Jesus told a story that warned people to be good while they are alive, or they might suffer after they die.

There was once a rich man who wore expensive clothes, ate fine food, and lived in complete luxury. There was also a poor man named Lazarus, whose body was covered with sores. Often, Lazarus would go to the rich man's door, hoping to be given any scraps of food that fell from the rich man's table. But nothing was given to him, and he always went away without even the smallest crumb.

When Lazarus died, angels took him up to Heaven, where he sat beside Abraham. Later, the rich man died and was buried. But instead of going to Heaven, he went to Hell. It was a hot and frightening place to be, and when he looked up, the rich man could see Abraham and Lazarus sitting together in Heaven.

The rich man called out to Abraham, "Father Abraham, please take pity on me and send Lazarus to bring me a drop of cool water. I'm burning hot and terrified at being so close to this lake of roasting fire."

Abraham answered, "My son, you had many good things during your life, but Lazarus experienced only poverty and pain. Now he is comfortable and you are suffering. There is a great divide between us, so we cannot cross over to you - and you cannot cross over to us."

The rich man replied, "Then please will you send Lazarus to my father's house to warn my five brothers, so that they will not be sent here, too."

"But your brothers have Moses and all the prophets to warn them," Abraham replied.

"That's not enough, father Abraham!" replied the rich man. "If someone who had risen from the dead spoke to them, they would realize they should not live such selfish lives."

Abraham shook his head, "I'm sorry. If they will not listen to Moses and the prophets, they will not be convinced by someone who has risen from the dead."

Did you know?

Heaven is also called Paradise, and Hell is also called Hades.

Lazarus Lives!

John 11:25 Jesus said to her, "I am the resurrection and the life. Whoever believes in me will live, even though he dies."

Jesus had many friends. Three of his closest friends were a brother and two sisters, named Lazarus, Martha, and Mary. Jesus often visited their home in Bethany, a small town about half an hour's walk from Jerusalem.

One day, Lazarus became ill, and the doctor said there was nothing he could do for him. Both sisters looked at each other in despair. "Jesus could make him better," said Mary.

"Let's send a message asking him to help," said Martha.

Jesus was far away, and it took days for the message to reach him. The disciples who told Jesus the bad news could see that he was concerned.

By the time Jesus finally reached Bethany, Lazarus had been dead for four days and was already buried. Martha went to meet Jesus while Mary stayed at home.

"Jesus, if you had only been here, my brother would not have died," Martha cried.

"Listen, Martha," said Jesus. "Even though he has died, your brother will live again. Do you believe this?"

"Yes, I believe you because I know that you are God's son,"she replied.

Martha went back and told Mary that Jesus wanted to see her, too. So Mary left the house and went to meet Jesus. When she saw him, Mary said the same as Martha, "If you had been here, Lazarus would not have died."

Mary was crying, along with many of the friends who had come with her. Jesus also cried.

"Where have you buried your brother?" asked Jesus.

Mary and her friends led Jesus to where Lazarus had been buried, in a cave with a stone over the opening. "Take the stone away," ordered Jesus.

When the stone had been removed, Jesus prayed aloud to God, "Thank you, Father, for always listening to my prayers. May everyone now see that you have sent me to give life." Then Jesus called, "Lazarus! Come out!"

A tense silence followed and nobody breathed. Then Lazarus emerged, wrapped in the cloths he had been buried in, and he stumbled out of the cold cave and into the bright sunshine.

Jesus said, "Help Lazarus out of those grave clothes."

Everyone surged forward, overjoyed to help Lazarus, who had died but was alive once more.

Did you know?

This miracle made some people worry about Jesus' powers, believing he could be dangerous.

Jesus Enters Jerusalem

John 12:12-13 The next day a great crowd who had come to the feast heard that Jesus was coming to Jerusalem. So they took branches of palm trees and went out to meet him.

In preparation for the eight-day Passover festival, the city of Jerusalem was bustling. All kinds of people were flocking there from far and wide, and the narrow streets were alive with the latest story about Jesus. It was said that he had brought a man back to life who had been dead and buried for four days! Then the news spread that Jesus was on his way to Jerusalem. An excited crowd set off to meet him.

Meanwhile, Jesus and his disciples had reached a village some way from Jerusalem. Jesus asked two of his disciples to go into the village and bring him a young donkey that was tethered there. "If anyone asks what you are doing," said Jesus, "tell them that the Master needs him and will send him back soon."

"Hey! What are you doing?" shouted a man as the disciples untied the donkey. "The Master wants him," replied the disciples.

"That's fine, then," replied the man. "But be careful with him; no one has ever ridden that donkey before."

The disciples spread their cloaks on the donkey's back to make a saddle for Jesus. As soon as Jesus climbed on to the young donkey's back, it was calm and stepped forward proudly.

Many years before this, the prophet Zechariah had foretold that one day the true king would come to Jerusalem, not galloping on a horse, but riding peacefully on a donkey. People knew this, and everyone who saw Jesus on that day believed that he was the true king.

A large crowd hurried to join Jesus and his disciples as they entered Jerusalem. Some went ahead, and some even threw down their cloaks so that the donkey could walk over them. Others cut down palm branches from the trees and spread them on the road as the donkey carried Jesus slowly into the city.

"Hosanna!" shouted the people. "Here comes our long-promised king! God bless the one who comes in the name of the Lord!"

On through the streets the crowd went, to the beautiful temple where Jews from all over the world gathered to praise God.

Did you know?

Passover celebrates the freeing of the Hebrews from captivity in Egypt. The Angel of Death killed the firstborn in Egyptian homes but "passed over" Hebrew homes.

Jesus in the Temple

Luke 19:45-46 Then he went into the temple and began driving out the traders, with these words: "Scripture says, 'My house shall be a house of prayer' – but you have made it a robbers' den."

Jesus arrived at the courtyard of the temple. He looked around, but since it was evening and Jerusalem was so crowded, he and his disciples went back to Bethany to stay with friends for the night.

The following morning, Jesus and his disciples returned to Jerusalem and Jesus went straight back to the temple. Although the big courtyard was open to all, it should have been a quiet place where people could come to pray and learn about God. Instead, there was a terrible noise. Animals bleated and mooed, birds twittered, market traders shouted, and people crossed the courtyard with their animals, using it as a shortcut.

Jesus could see that the traders were selling animals to pilgrims to use as offerings to God, and they were charging many times the normal price for them. The money-changers were cheating, too. Every Jew had to pay a "temple tax" at Passover time, but those who changed the pilgrims' coins were making a big profit. Some people believed that the priests themselves were behind much of the trading.

Jesus was very angry. The poor were being cheated, and God's house was being used as a corrupt market. Fearlessly, he strode forward and shooed away the oxen, sheep, and doves, then he began overturning all the tables, scattering coins everywhere. Next, he turned away the people who were using the temple as a shortcut through the streets of the town.

Everyone stopped in their tracks as Jesus exclaimed, "How dare these people trade in the temple? They should sell their goods elsewhere! Thieves and money-changers have no place in a house of prayer!"

Pilgrims looked on in amazement. Jesus was being incredibly brave, defying some of the most powerful people in the land. The priests and leaders were furious with Jesus. It was their job to keep order in the temple, not his, but they were wary of him because so many people followed him and believed that he was the Son of God.

The traders had a reason to be cross with Jesus because, under the Law of Moses, people were required to offer animal sacrifices. Those journeying a long way to the temple in Jerusalem would take money with them to buy an animal for their offering. So it was not wrong for men to sell the animals, but people knew that Jesus was right that they should have been selling them outside the temple area.

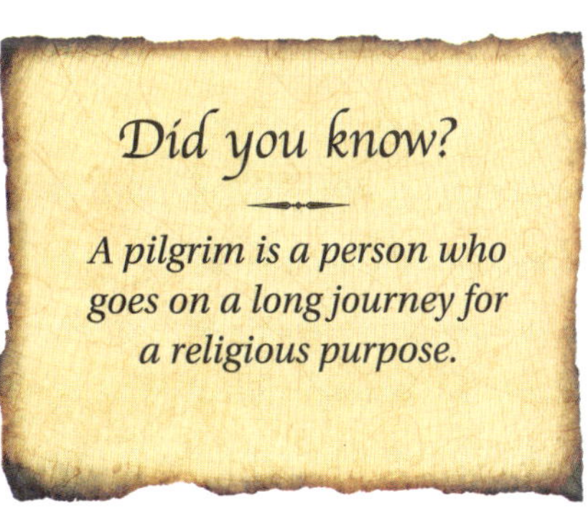

Jesus and the Pharisees

Matthew 23:13 "How terrible for you, teachers of the law and Pharisees! You hypocrites! You lock the door to the kingdom of Heaven in people's faces."

After clearing the money-changers and merchants out of the Temple, Jesus spent the night in Bethany, a nearby village. The next day, he went back to the Temple. This time, the Pharisees set a trap for him. They sent some of their disciples to ask Jesus whether it was right for Jews to pay taxes to the Romans. They knew that if he said "yes," he would be very unpopular. If he said "no," he would be encouraging people to break the Roman law.

Jesus saw through them at once. He asked for a coin and then asked whose name and face were on it. "The Roman emperor's," he was told. "Then give the emperor what belongs to him," said Jesus, "and don't forget to give God what is due to him as well."

There were, as always, crowds of people in the Temple, as well as the Pharisees and the teachers of the law. Speaking first to the people, Jesus told them that they should obey the law teachers and Pharisees, but that they should not follow their examples as these people did not do as they preached. They were hypocrites!

Did you know?

The Pharisees were also known as "chasidim," which means loyal to God, or loved of God. However, they were actually the fiercest opponents of Jesus Christ and his message.

"Take a look at yourselves," Jesus told the law teachers and the Pharisees. "You have scripture verses on your clothing, and you carry around books of God's word, yet you would not help your fellow man."

The religious leaders bowed their heads with embarrassment when Jesus continued. "These so-called men of God always take the best places at feasts and at the synagogue for themselves. They cannot properly encourage people to live good lives, since they themselves do not live properly."

Jesus scolded the religious men for robbing the poor, acting unfairly, and for following the laws of evil instead of the laws of the temple. He condemned them for making themselves seem good by giving God gifts and riches, while at the same time turning their backs on such important values as justice, honesty, and mercy.

As the scribes, law teachers, and Pharisees shuffled their feet and looked at the ground, Jesus turned to address the crowd, "These men might look like they are good people on the outside, but inside they are rotten!"

Finally, Jesus told the law teachers and Pharisees that they would be punished for their hypocrisy.

The Last Supper

Mark 14:25 "I tell you, I will never again drink this wine until the day I drink the new wine in the Kingdom of God."

At the end of the Passover celebrations, it was time for the Passover meal. Jesus knew that his enemies were looking for him, so he needed to share his Passover meal in secrecy with his friends. During the day, the disciples asked where Jesus wanted to have the meal, as Jerusalem was overcrowded. But many people were happy to share their homes with Jesus, and he had already made plans.

In reply to his disciples, Jesus said, "Go to the city and find a man carrying a jar of water. He will lead you to a house. Ask the owner of the house to show you the room upstairs where you can prepare the meal, and we will eat there."

The disciples easily found the man carrying the water – usually only women carried water. Everything happened as Jesus had told them, and they prepared their meal in the upstairs room of the house.

That evening, Jesus and his disciples sat down in the room. In those days, the least important servant washed the feet of guests who had walked along dusty roads. A jug of water and towel lay ready, but no servants were present and not one of the disciples was prepared to do such a lowly job.

Jesus poured some hot water into a basin and picked up the towel. Then he knelt before each disciple and washed their feet.

When Jesus had finished his task, he said, "You see? I am prepared to do anything for you. You must be ready, too – to serve each other. Don't always think of yourselves and your own importance."

Later, as they sat at the table eating, drinking, and talking, Jesus looked around, smiled sadly, and said, "One of you will betray me to my enemies."

The disciples were horrified. "You can't mean me?" asked each one.

When one of the disciples, Judas Iscariot, asked this, Jesus replied, "Yes, you are the one." Then he broke a piece of bread and shared it with everyone. "This is my body," he said. "When you break and eat bread together like this, remember me."

Then Jesus passed a cup of wine among them. "Drink this, all of you," he said. "This is my blood, which will be poured out so that everyone's sins can be forgiven by God."

Did you know?

Today, people celebrate Passover by eating "matzo," a flat bread similar to the bread that the Israelites ate after their quick departure from Egypt.

The Garden of Gethsemane

Luke 22:48 Jesus said, "Judas, is it with a kiss that you betray the Son of Man?"

Jesus and the disciples finished the Passover meal and went for a walk to a quiet place outside the city.

"You will all run away from me," Jesus told them.

"Never!" exclaimed Peter. "I'd die with you if necessary."

The others all agreed.

Jesus shook his head. "Peter," he said, "before the cock crows tomorrow, three times you will have said that you don't know me."

"Never!" repeated Peter.

Jesus and his disciples reached a garden named Gethsemane.

Gathering his disciples, Jesus said, "Wait here while I pray. I am very sad. Please keep watch for me."

Walking a short distance away from the others, Jesus threw himself on the ground. "Please, Father!" he prayed, "don't let me suffer!"

After praying for a while longer, Jesus spoke again, this time more calmly, "Don't do what I want, but do what you know is best."

Some time later, Jesus walked slowly back to his friends, who had fallen asleep. "Couldn't you have stayed awake just for one more hour?" he asked, disappointed. "Now you will have to wake up because I'm going to be taken prisoner. Look! Here comes the one who has betrayed me."

The disciples woke and rubbed their eyes. A rough-looking crowd, including temple guards armed with sticks and spears, were walking toward them. At the front of the crowd was Judas Iscariot.

"The man I kiss is the one you want," Judas whispered to the guards.

Judas walked boldly up to Jesus. "Hello, Teacher," he said, and kissed him on the cheek.

Jesus looked at Judas. "My friend," he said sadly, "are you betraying me with a kiss?"

Peter was furious as the guards rushed forward and seized Jesus. Pulling out a sword, Peter lashed out wildly, cutting off one of the guard's ears.

"Put your sword away, Peter!" said Jesus. "If I wished to go free, I could call armies of angels to fight for me. But I am ready to give up my life according to God's plan."

Gently, Jesus reached out and touched the guard's bleeding ear, which healed instantly. Then he said to his captors, "Why are you treating me like a criminal? Every day, I sat teaching in the Temple, but you didn't arrest me then." The man did not answer.

Jesus knew that the priests who had him arrested were afraid of the crowds of people who followed him. But there were no crowds now. As he was taken out of the garden, the terrified disciples ran away from him.

Did you know?

The garden of Gethsemane is at the foot of the Mount of Olives in Jerusalem.

Peter Denies Jesus

Luke 22:56-57 She said: "This man was with him, too," but he denied it, saying, "Woman, I do not know him."

The guards took Jesus to the house of Caiaphas, the high priest. It was still evening, but the priests had decided that they must put Jesus on trial at once and avoid trouble from his many followers who were in Jerusalem at the time.

Meanwhile, Peter and another disciple had stopped running. They suddenly realized how cowardly they were being and decided to follow the guards to see the place where Jesus was being taken.

When Peter and his companion reached the house of Caiaphas, they asked a servant girl at the gate if they could go in. "Yes," she answered, then looked closely at Peter. "Aren't you a disciple of that man?" she asked, pointing toward a room where Jesus had been taken.

"No, I am not!" replied Peter, afraid that he might be arrested for earlier cutting a guard's ear with his sword. He shivered and made his way to warm his hands at the hot coal fire in the courtyard. A man standing nearby stared at Peter. "Aren't you one of that man's disciples?" he asked.

Afraid of what might happen to him if others overheard, Peter bowed his head and replied, "No, I am not!"

In the corner of the courtyard, servants were discussing the latest events. They looked across at Peter, and one called across, "You are one of the prisoner's friends. You can't deny it, I saw you with him – and you come from Galilee, too. You have the same accent!"

Everyone stared at Peter, who lost his temper. "I tell you, I don't know who you're talking about," he shouted.

Just then, dawn began to light up the dark sky, and somewhere nearby, a cock crowed. With a shudder, Peter remembered what Jesus had said to him just a few hours earlier, "Before the cock crows tomorrow, three times you will have said that you don't know me."

Ashamed with himself, Peter looked through the window to where Jesus was standing, being questioned by his enemies. Jesus looked back at him kindly. Peter felt terrible. He had failed someone who had never let him down. He rushed out of the courtyard crying bitterly.

Did you know?

Peter is one of the most important of Jesus' twelve disciples, and Jesus calls him his "rock." He was the first to call Jesus "the Messiah," which means "anointed by God."

The Trial of Jesus

Mark 15:9-10 "Do you want me to set free for you the king of the Jews?" He knew very well that the chief priests had handed Jesus over to him because they were jealous.

Jesus was on trial before the Council of Jewish leaders. He was blindfolded and beaten by the guards. The council called in several witnesses to prove that he was guilty of many things, but none of the witnesses told the same story. Angry, the high priest, Caiaphas, demanded, "Are you the Son of God?"

"I am," replied Jesus.

"Ha!" answered Caiaphas. "We don't need anymore witnesses. He has said he is like a god, and for this, he deserves to die."

But the Jewish leaders weren't allowed to put people to death. Only the Romans could do that, so Jesus was sent to the Roman governor, a man named Pontius Pilate. As Jesus stood before Pilate in chains, the priests warned, "This troublemaker tells people not to pay taxes and says he is their king."

If this was true, Jesus could be sentenced to death, but Pilate was sure that the religious leaders had made up the charges because they were jealous of Jesus.

"Are you the king of the Jews?" Pilate asked. But Jesus would answer no more of his questions.

Pilate was sure that Jesus was innocent, but outside his palace, the priests were stirring up trouble. A large crowd of people were now chanting, "Crucify him!"

Pilate had an idea. "It's Passover," he called to the unruly mob. "As part of the celebrations, I always set one prisoner free. This man has done nothing to deserve death, so shall he be set free?"

But the priests had placed their own people in the crowd with orders to tell everyone what to say. "No!" they all yelled. "Free Barabbas, instead!" Barabbas was in prison for murder. Pilate shrugged and ordered his soldiers to set Barabbas free.

Meanwhile, other soldiers beat Jesus cruelly and made him a crown of thorny twigs. They forced it on his head, wrapped a purple cloak around him, and jeered, "Long live the King!"

At last, Pilate took Jesus out to the crowd. The priests had done their work, and as soon as the crowd saw Jesus, they roared, "Let him die on the cross!"

And so, the same people who had welcomed Jesus into Jerusalem only five days before had demanded his death.

Did you know?

Crucifixion was supposed to shame the person being executed and warn onlookers not to do what that person had done.

The Crucifixion

Mark 15:39 And the curtain of the temple was torn in two from top to bottom. And when the centurion who was standing opposite him saw how he died, he said, "Truly this man was a son of God."

Jesus was led away to die. Under Jewish law, he had to be killed outside the city gates. The Roman soldiers made him carry the heavy wooden cross to a place called Golgotha. A mocking crowd followed, and Jesus, weak from being questioned and beaten, stumbled beneath the weight of the cross.

A broad-shouldered man named Simon, who had come from North Africa for Passover, was there, and the soldiers grabbed him. "Carry the cross for the prisoner!" they called, "or we'll never get there." Simon helped Jesus for the rest of the way to Golgotha. Then the words "The King of the Jews" were written on the cross.

When they reached the hill, the soldiers laid Jesus down on the cross and hammered nails through his feet and wrists. Jesus said, "Father forgive them, for they do not realize what they are doing."

Two robbers were put on crosses on either side of him. The crosses were set into the ground and lifted up, so that the men would die from heat and thirst. It was nine o'clock in the morning, so the soldiers sat down and began gambling with dice to pass the time until the prisoners died.

When the religious leaders arrived, they taunted, "You saved others, but you can't save yourself."

Then one of the two robbers called out, "Aren't you the Chosen One? Save yourself and us!"

"Don't say that," interrupted the other second robber. "We are both getting what we deserve, but this man has done nothing wrong!" Then turning toward Jesus, he said, "Remember me when you reach your kingdom."

"Today you will be with me in Paradise," replied Jesus.

Some of Jesus' friends were there, crying. Jesus whispered down to John, "Look after my mother and be a son to her."

At noon, when the sun should have been at its brightest, the sky turned black and Jesus called out, "My God, why have you deserted me?" By three o'clock, he gasped, "I'm so thirsty!"

A soldier soaked a sponge in sour wine and held it up to moisten Jesus' dry lips. Then in a clear voice, Jesus said, "It's finished!"

At that moment, back in Jerusalem, the curtain in the temple was torn in two. At Golgotha, Jesus bowed his head and died.

Did you know?

The name Christ comes from the Greek word "Christos," meaning anointed or chosen one. "Messiah" means the same thing.

Jesus Rises from the Grave

Mark 16:10-11 She went and told his companions. They were mourning and crying, and when they heard her say that Jesus was alive and that she had seen him, they did not believe her.

Two of Jesus' followers asked Pontius Pilate if they could give Jesus a proper burial. When Pilate agreed, they took his body, wrapped it in strips of cloth, and took it to a garden where a new grave had been cut into a rock. The Pharisees were worried that the disciples would steal the body and pretend that Jesus had risen, so they made sure that the tomb was sealed, and Roman soldiers stood guard so no one could go near it.

Some of the women who had been Jesus's friends had watched the burial. Worn out with sadness and crying, they went away. It was Friday evening and the next day was the Sabbath, the Jewish day of rest. None of the friends and disciples could do anything but mourn and wait for the Sabbath to be over.

As soon as Saturday evening came, the women began preparing perfumes and spices to put on Jesus' body. It was the only way they felt they could show how much they cared for Jesus.

Very early on the Sunday morning, Mary Magdalene, with some of the other women, made their way to the garden. But when they arrived, they could not believe their eyes. The guards had gone, and the huge rock that had sealed the grave had been moved aside, leaving the tomb wide open.

Mary Magdalene ran to get Peter and John. When they returned, they peered inside the cave. On the floor lay the grave cloths and Jesus' body had gone. Peter and John couldn't understand it and went back to the other disciples. Mary remained, tears pouring down her cheeks. She turned, looking into the tomb again, and saw two angels sitting where Jesus' body had been.

"Why are you crying?" asked a man's voice. She had not noticed anyone else in the garden and supposed that he was the gardener. "Sir," she replied, "they have moved Jesus' body. Do you know where it is?"

"Mary!" exclaimed the man, and suddenly she recognized him. It was Jesus.

"Master!" she cried.

"Go and tell my disciples that I have risen and am on my way to our Father," said Jesus, smiling.

Mary ran out of the garden, her sadness lifted. She burst in on the grieving group of disciples and cried, "He's alive! He's really alive!"

Did you know?

The Jewish Sabbath is from sunset on Friday to sunset on Saturday. This was because God created the world by the sixth day, and on the seventh day he rested.

Jesus Visits His Disciples

Luke 24:30-31 As he sat down to eat with them, he took some bread, blessed it and broke it, and gave it to them. And their eyes were opened, and they knew him; and he vanished out of their sight.

On the afternoon when Jesus rose again, two of Jesus' disciples walked to their home in the nearby village of Emmaus when a stranger caught up with them. "You look sad," he said. "What's wrong?"

"Haven't you heard about Jesus of Nazareth?" asked one of the disciples. "We thought that he had been sent by God, but he's been put to death."

"Some women are saying that they've seen him alive, but he had definitely died when they took him down from the cross," said the second disciple.

"Now his body has disappeared from his tomb," added the first.

The stranger replied, "But don't our holy writings say that God's promised king must die and rise again?"

The stranger continued talking about the meanings of the scriptures, and in no time, they had reached the disciples' home in Emmaus.

"Come in, stranger!" urged the disciples. "Have supper with us."

The man accepted, and at the table, he thanked God and passed the bread around. Suddenly, the disciples recognized the stranger. It was Jesus!

Excited by what they had seen, the two men rushed back to Jerusalem to tell the other disciples what they had seen. Before they could say anything, the disciples cried "Jesus has risen! Peter has seen him!" Then the two men told the other disciples they had met Jesus, too.

Suddenly, Jesus was in the room. He sat with all the disciples and explained that soon they would have to tell everyone that he had died and come alive again, so that the sins of mankind could be forgiven.

The Miraculous Catch of Fish

John 21:6 And he said to them, "Cast your net on the right side of the boat, and see what you find." When they did so, they were not able to pull the net up, there were so many fish in it.

One evening in Galilee, Peter went fishing with James, John, Thomas, and some of the other disciples.

But as night passed and daybreak came, they hadn't caught a single fish. Across on the shore, a man cupped his hands and called across the lake to them, "Cast your net to the right!"

Something about him made the disciples obey. They tossed their net to the right, and at once it was weighed down with fish.

"That's Jesus!" John said to Peter. Peter leapt into the water and swam! By the time he reached the shore, Jesus was already cooking some fish.

"Bring more fish!" said Jesus, so Peter went to meet the boat and helped to haul the heavy net ashore.

When the friends counted the fish, there were one hundred and fifty-three! The disciples hungrily ate the bread and grilled fish that Jesus had prepared, then Peter walked along the shore with Jesus.

Three times, Jesus asked Peter the same question, "Peter, do you love me?"

Peter felt ashamed, remembering how he had lied three times about knowing Jesus. "Yes," answered Peter, sadly.

"Then look after my followers," said Jesus.

Peter realized that Jesus had forgiven him because he had given him an important job to do.

The Ascension

Acts 1:11 This Jesus, who has been taken away from you up to Heaven, will come in the same way as you have seen him go.

For forty days, Jesus appeared to his friends at different times. He looked and seemed different, but there was no doubt that he was alive. He ate meals with the disciples and talked with them as he had before he was crucified. He helped the disciples to understand a lot more about the scriptures than they had before. But now he could pass through closed doors and appear or disappear at will.

On the fortieth day after he had risen in the garden, he walked with them to the Mount of Olives and turned to them. "You must tell everyone all about what has happened," he said. "Go and preach the Gospel everywhere, and make your own disciples, baptizing them in the name of the Father, the Son, and the Holy Spirit. Once people understand why I suffered and died, then rose again, they will live better lives."

Jesus held up his hands to bless them and spoke once more. "Remember that I will be with you always, just as I always told you." Then he rose up into the sky and disappeared behind a cloud. The disciples returned to Jerusalem and went to the temple every day to thank God for Jesus.

One morning, six weeks later, Jerusalem was once more packed with pilgrims, who had all come to celebrate the festival of Pentecost, the harvest thanksgiving for the first ripe crops.

Something strange happened. The disciples were in a house, when a great rushing wind suddenly blew through the rooms. Then, just for an instant, separate little tongues of flame settled on every disciple. Warmth surged through them, and they realized that this was the Holy Spirit, sent to them from Heaven.

A large crowd had gathered outside the house. The people had seen and heard the wind and wondered what was happening. The disciples stepped outside, feeling happy for the first time in weeks. What happened then was even more amazing. Everyone in the street, no matter what country they had come from, understood perfectly what the disciples were saying.

Did you know?

Pentecost is a Greek name for the Israelite Harvest Festival. It means "fiftieth" – the feast was held fifty days after Passover.

The Early Church

Acts 3:8 And jumping up, he stood on his feet and walked. Then he went into the temple with them, walking, leaping, and praising God.

Peter and the other disciples taught more people about Jesus, baptizing them as Jesus had done. Thousands of people became new disciples and met in each other's houses to pray together. Their happiness spread, and even more people began joining them.

One afternoon, Peter and John were going to the Temple when they met a lame beggar. He sat beside the temple gates each day, calling "Give me some money! I can't walk. Give me some money so that I can buy food!"

Peter and John stopped. They saw this man every day but had not yet spoken to him.

"I haven't any money to give you," said Peter, "but I'll give you what I have. In the name of Jesus Christ, get up and walk!"

Peter helped the beggar to stand, and at once, the beggar felt strength flow into his feet and ankles. He let go of Peter's hand and started to walk. Then he began running and jumping, shouting, "Look, I can walk! How good God is. Thank you, God!"

The beggar ran into the temple where everyone who knew him was amazed to see him walking about and praising God.

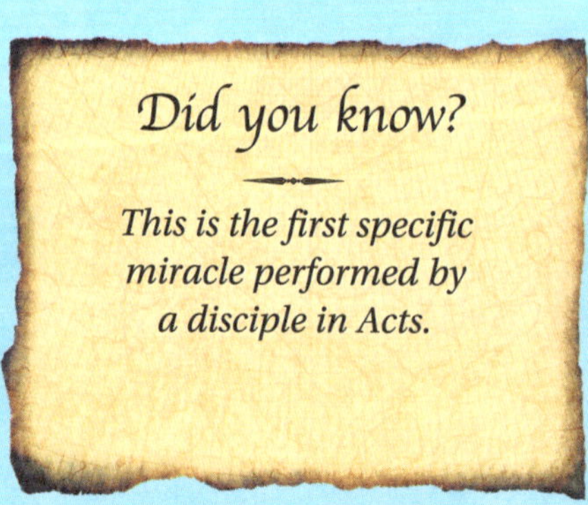

The First Martyr

Acts 7:60 Then he fell on his knees and cried aloud, "Lord, do not hold this sin against them." And with that he died.

The disciples helped whoever wanted or needed it, but so much time was taken up with caring for the needy, that they did not have enough time to preach and pray as Jesus had asked them to do.

Eventually, the disciples picked seven men to be in charge of sharing the funds they raised among those who needed help.

One of the men was named Stephen, who argued with the Pharisees very well to prove that Jesus was the Messiah. This infuriated them. "He must be stopped!" they said. "He is going against the way we've followed God for centuries."

The Pharisees made up false charges against him and put him on trial.

Bravely, Stephen stood before the Pharisees and said, "You rejected and murdered Jesus, God's own son." This made the Pharisees angry, and they threatened to kill Stephen, too.

Stephen simply said, "I can see Jesus in Heaven, standing at God's side." At this, the leaders, including a young Pharisee named Saul, dragged him out of the city. They picked up stones and hurled them at Stephen. Falling to his knees, he prayed, "Lord Jesus, take me to you!"

Just before he died, Stephen said, "Forgive them for this crime."

Did you know?

The name Stephen comes from a Greek word meaning "crown."

Saul Is Converted

Acts 9:5 "Saul, Saul, why do you persecute me?" "Tell me, Lord," he said, "who you are." The voice answered, "I am Jesus."

Saul was proud to be a Pharisee and was determined to stop people following Jesus. One day, he set off on the road to Damascus to try and capture some of Jesus' supporters and bring them back to Jerusalem. On the way, a dazzling light shone all around him and made him blind.

From nowhere, he heard a voice, "Saul, why are you attacking me?"

Terrified, Saul asked, "Who are you?"

"I am Jesus," came the reply. "When you attack my followers, you attack me."

"What do you want me to do, Lord?" Saul asked, his hatred gone.

"Go to Damascus and you will be told," said Jesus.

The men who were accompanying Saul to Damascus were puzzled and wondered who Saul was talking to; although they could hear a voice, they couldn't see anyone there. Realizing that he was unable to see, they led Saul to a house in Damascus, where he stayed for three days, blind and also neither eating nor drinking.

Jesus appeared in a vision to one of his followers, a man named Ananias, and told him to go to see Saul. Ananias was horrified to hear this. "But Saul is our enemy," he said.

Jesus explained that he had chosen Saul to become his follower, so Ananias went to the house where Saul was staying and spoke kindly to him. At once, Saul felt a strange sensation, as though something like fish scales were falling from his eyes – and suddenly he could see again! Then Ananias baptized him as a sign that he now followed Jesus.

Saul began to tell everyone he could about God and Jesus, but this made Saul's own people become his bitter enemies. They watched the city gates, planning to catch him and kill him. But one night, Saul's new friends lowered him over the city walls in a basket and he escaped.

Did you know?

Saul was a clever man who spoke Greek and Latin. He was also known by the Latin and Greek name "Paul."

Paul Is Taken Captive

Acts 16:33 At that very hour of the night, the jailer took them and washed their wounds; and he and all his family were baptized at once.

In Antioch, Syria, followers of Christ were called "Christians." Two missionaries, Paul (formerly named Saul) and his friend Barnabas, went to tell the new believers more about Jesus. After a year there, God told them to go and teach about Jesus in other countries.

Wherever they visited, many Jews attacked them. Still, they continued their journey and preached for many years. Eventually, Paul and Barnabas separated, and Paul went abroad with a new companion named Silas.

In one country, they met a slave girl who could tell people's fortunes. Paul knew that the girl's powers came from an evil spirit and not from God. Through Jesus, Paul freed her of the evil spirit, and her magic powers left her.

The girl's masters were furious, for they could no longer make money out of her. They dragged Paul and Silas to the authorities, where they were chained to the prison walls.

That night, an earthquake shook the prison. The doors flew open and chains broke loose from the walls. Sure that he would be blamed for the escape of the prisoners, the prison officer drew a sword to kill himself.

"Don't do it! We're still here!" called Paul.

The prison officer fell down on his knees. "What must I do now?" he asked.

"Believe in Jesus, and God will save you and your family." said Paul.

The prison officer prayed to Jesus and then took Paul and Silas to his house.

Shipwrecked

Acts 27:20 For days on end, there was no sign of either sun or stars, a great storm was raging, and our last hopes of coming through alive began to fade.

Years later, while preaching Jesus' teachings in Jerusalem, Paul was arrested again. People were suspicious about this new religion. Knowing he was innocent, Paul asked that the Roman emperor should hear his case. As he was a Roman citizen, his captors had to allow this.

Paul was sent to Rome on a ship, guarded by Roman soldiers. It was almost winter and the winds were rough. Paul said to the captain, "Don't sail any farther, or we will all face disaster." But the captain ignored him.

They had just set sail when a fierce storm began to rage. Heavy seas lashed the decks, and the crew fought to keep the ship under control for several days and nights.

Then Paul called everyone together. "God has told me that we will all reach Rome," he said. "The ship will be lost, but we will all be safe."

Two weeks after the storm began, the sailors dropped anchor close to land. As the sun began to rise, they saw a stretch of unknown coastline and tried to guide the ship toward it. Instead, it hit a sandbank and began to break up, smashed by the heavy waves. Everyone jumped into the sea and swam to shore, and they all reached land safely, just as God had told Paul they would.

Did you know?

Paul was actually shipwrecked a total of three times.

Paul's Letters

Romans 12:21 Do not let evil conquer you, but do good to defeat evil.

Wherever Paul preached, those who heard him came together to form a church. Paul chose leaders for these new churches and taught the Christians all he knew. When he left them, Paul wrote letters to encourage them to continue teaching Jesus' word.

When Paul was put in prison for preaching, he had more time for letter writing. One day, he wrote to his friend, Philemon.

"This letter comes with your slave, Onesimus. He ran away from you, and I am sending him back. He has been a great comfort to me in prison, and I wish he could stay with me, but I know he will be useful to you. He has become a Christian, which means that he is now your brother as well as your slave, so please welcome him back. If he stole any money from you, I will pay it back for him. I know you will do as I ask."

Philemon thought of Paul, chained up in prison, and reread the letter. Then he turned to Onesimus and said, "Welcome home!"

One of Paul's last letters was to his old friend, Timothy.

"Be strong and bear all difficulties like Jesus. Don't be tempted away from what you know, but always be fair, honest, peaceful, and caring."

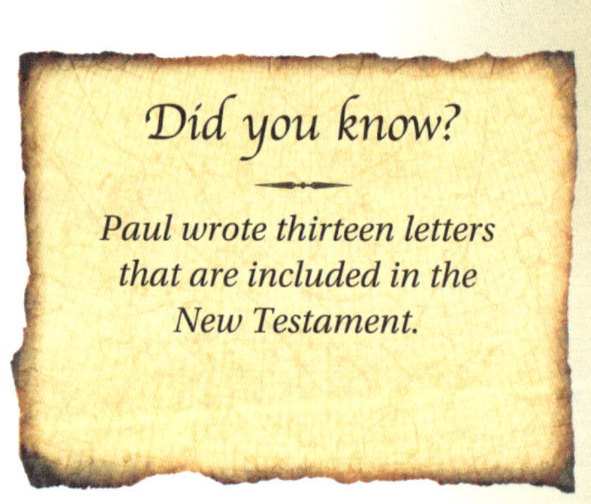

Did you know?

Paul wrote thirteen letters that are included in the New Testament.

God Shows Peter the Way

Acts 10:14-15 Peter said, "Not so, Lord; for I have never eaten anything that is common or unclean." And the voice spoke to him a second time, saying, "What God has cleansed, you shall not call common."

One day, Peter had a dream. Animals were coming down from the sky, and God told Peter to kill one of the animals for his dinner. When Peter saw that the animals were all of the kind that Jews are forbidden to eat by their law, he said, "Certainly not! I've never eaten an unclean animal in my life!"

"Everything that I make is good, Peter," said God.

This happened three times, and then Peter woke up. He was trying to figure out what his dream meant, when he remembered he was meeting with Cornelius, a Roman centurion, who wanted to learn more about Jesus.

Jews were not allowed to mix with foreigners, but Peter remembered his dream. And now he understood – in God's eyes, there are no differences between people.

Cornelius prayed to God and was kind to the poor. The day before Peter's dream, an angel had appeared to him, telling him to send for Peter, who would teach him more.

When Peter arrived at his house, Cornelius fell to his knees, but Peter said, "Don't kneel. I'm just like you." Then Peter spoke to all the people gathered there, telling them, "Everyone is the same in God's eyes."

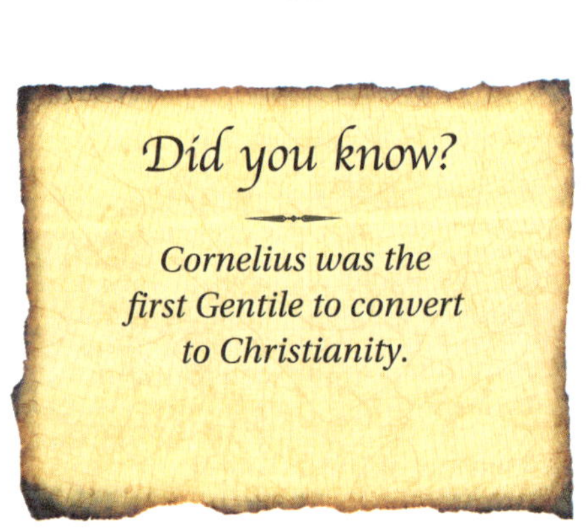

Did you know?

Cornelius was the first Gentile to convert to Christianity.

John's Vision

Revelation 21:21 The twelve gates were twelve pearls, each gate being made from a single pearl. The streets of the city were of pure gold, like translucent glass.

Many Christians were punished for being followers of Jesus. One of them, John, was arrested for preaching the gospel and was sent to live on the small island of Patmos in Greece. John was old now, and he was lonely, but he still loved and praised Jesus.

One day, John heard a voice in the air. He saw Jesus, surrounded by seven golden candlesticks. In his right hand, Jesus held seven stars.

"Do not be afraid," said Jesus. "I was dead, but now I am alive forever. These seven stars and the seven candlesticks represent seven churches. I have a message for each."

The churches, which were in the Roman province of Asia, were in different cities that were linked by an important road through the richest and busiest areas.

John wrote down the messages to the seven churches as Jesus told him, "I know you haven't given up your faith, but some of you do not love me as much as you did, and you have started doing some things wrong. Stop this and listen to my Holy Spirit."

The seventh message, to the church in the city of Laodicea, was similar to the first six, but Jesus spoke more sternly, "You think you are strong and powerful, but really you are poor and weak because you do not rely on me. Turn back to me; I will give you all you need. I am always just outside your door. Open the door and let me in."

After this, Jesus showed John what Heaven is like. John saw someone glowing like precious jewels, sitting on a throne of glittering glass and gold. A brilliant rainbow curved around the throne, and seven fiery torches surrounded it.

John realized that however much the Roman emperor or other rulers tried to hurt Christians, God was really in control.

Then, Jesus showed John a beautiful bride on her way to her wedding. He said, "All sadness has vanished. God will wipe away your tears."

Finally, Jesus showed John a city, lit up and shining, with golden streets, gates of pearl, and a river of crystal. God and Jesus were there, shining even brighter than the city lights.

John understood that he was being shown the beginning of a new world, one that Jesus had made free of sin.

Jesus spoke once more, "There will be no more death, grief, crying, or pain. God's Holy City has no need of the sun or moon because the glory of God shines on it."

People and Places

Aaron Moses' brother. He was known to be a persuasive speaker.

Abarim Mountains A mountain range to the east of the Dead Sea.

Abednego One of three young men who were thrown into a furnace by King Nebuchadnezzar but were saved by God.

Abel The second son of Adam and Eve. He was killed by his brother Cain out of jealousy.

Abigail The wife of Nabal. After Nabal's death, she became David's wife.

Abimelech A son of Gideon. He killed his brothers and had himself proclaimed king, but he was himself killed in a rebellion.

Abraham The ancestor of the Israelites. He was the husband of Sarah and the father of Isaac.

Absalom The third son of King David. He rebelled against his father and was later killed by David's soldiers.

Adam The first human being created by God. He lived in the Garden of Eden.

Adonijah The fourth son of King David. He tried to seize the throne and eventually was put to death by his brother, King Solomon.

Ahab A king of Israel, the husband of Jezebel.

Ahaziah A king of Judah, the son of Queen Athaliah and father of King Joash.

Ai A city that was captured by the Israelites under Joshua.

Ammonites The descendants of Benammi, a son of Lot. They were enemies of the Israelites.

Amos The earliest of the prophets whose words are contained in a separate book of the Bible.

Amram The father of Moses, Aaron, and Miriam.

Andrew One of the first disciples of Jesus and one of the twelve apostles. He was Simon Peter's brother and, like him, a fisherman.

Antioch An ancient city in what is now southeast Turkey.

Archelaus One of Herod the Great's sons, who became the ruler of Judea after Herod died.

Asia A Roman province located in what is now western Turkey.

Assyria A powerful ancient kingdom in northern Mesopotamia (modern-day Iraq).

Athaliah The daughter of King Ahab and Queen Jezebel of Israel. She married King Jehoram of Judah.

Augustus The Roman emperor at the time of Jesus' birth.

Baal A Canaanite god.

Babylon An ancient city in southern Mesopotamia (modern-day Iraq).

Babylonia A powerful ancient kingdom in southern Mesopotamia (modern-day Iraq).

Balaam A prophet who was sent by Balak to curse the Israelites.

Balak A king of Moab.

Barabbas A bandit who was set free, instead of Jesus, by Pontius Pilate.

Barak An Israelite military leader who defeated Canaanite forces under Sisera.

Barnabas One of the earliest Christians. He frequently went on journeys with Paul.

Bartholomew One of the first disciples of Jesus and one of the twelve apostles.

Bathsheba The wife of Uriah, a commander in King David's army. David caused her husband's death in order to marry her.

Belshazzar The last king of Babylon.

Benjamin The youngest son of Jacob. *Also:* the name of the tribe descended from Benjamin.

Bethany The village near Jerusalem where Martha, Mary, and Lazarus lived.

Bethel A town near Jerusalem. Its name means "the house of God."

Bethlehem The town near Jerusalem where Jesus was born. Boaz and Ruth lived there, and King David was born there.

Bethuel A nephew of Abraham. His daughter Rebekah married Abraham's son Isaac.

Boaz A kind landowner who helped Ruth and Naomi, and then married Ruth.

Caiaphas The Jewish high priest who plotted to kill Jesus.

Cain The first son of Adam and Eve. He killed his brother Abel.

Caleb An Israelite leader at the time of Moses. He had a strong faith in God.

Cana A village in Galilee where Jesus performed his first miracle at a wedding.

Canaan The land God promised to the Israelites. It approximately covers modern-day Israel and Palestine.

Canaanites The people who were living in Canaan before the Israelites entered it, and who continued to live there.

Capernaum A town on the shore of the Sea of Galilee.

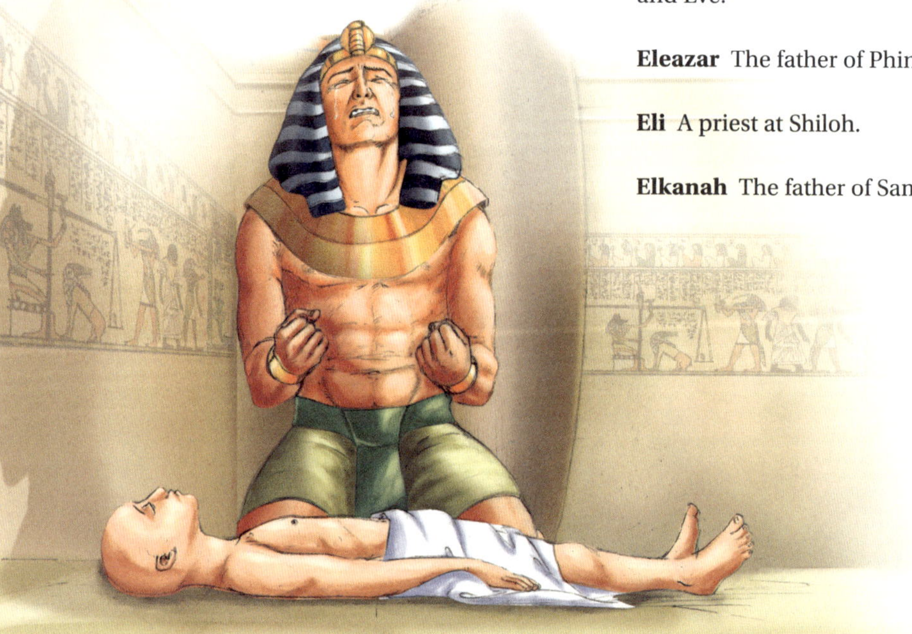

Cornelius A Roman centurion visited by Peter.

Dagon A Philistine god.

Damascus An ancient city, now the capital of Syria.

Daniel A Jewish captive in Babylon. He was thrown into a den of lions, but God saved him.

Darius A king of the Medes and Persians who conquered Babylon.

David The second king of Israel. As a young man, he killed the Philistine giant Goliath.

Dead Sea A large body of water between present-day Israel and Jordan.

Deborah A female prophet and Israelite leader.

Delilah Samson's second wife. She was bribed by the Philistines to find out the secret of Samson's strength.

Eden The garden created by God for Adam and Eve.

Eleazar The father of Phinehas.

Eli A priest at Shiloh.

Elkanah The father of Samuel.

Elijah A prophet of Israel. He opposed King Ahab and Queen Jezebel.

Elisha A prophet of Israel. He was also Elijah's successor.

Elizabeth The mother of John the Baptist.

Emmaus A village near Jerusalem.

Esau The elder son of Isaac and brother of Jacob.

Esther A Jewish wife of the Persian king Xerxes. She saved the Jews from a dangerous plot.

Eve The first woman created by God. God made her out of Adam's rib.

Ezekiel An Israelite prophet in Babylon.

Ezra A teacher of the Law of Moses.

Gabriel The archangel who foretold the births of Jesus and John to Mary and Elizabeth.

Gad The seventh son of Jacob. *Also:* the name of the tribe descended from Gad.

Galilee A region of northern Israel, west of the Sea of Galilee.

Garden of Gethsemane A garden on the Mount of Olives. Jesus went there to pray before he was captured and crucified.

Gibeon A Canaanite city.

Gideon A military leader who saved Israel from the Midianites.

Gilead Territory on the east side of the Jordan River, occupied by the tribes of Gad, Reuben, and some of Manasseh.

Gilgal A place near Jericho where the Israelites made a camp after crossing the Jordan.

Golgotha The hill near Jerusalem where Jesus was crucified.

Goliath The giant Philistine warrior killed by David.

Gomer The unfaithful wife of the prophet Hosea.

Gomorrah An ancient city destroyed, with Sodom, because of its wickedness.

Hades In ancient mythology, the place where people go when they die.

Hagar The Egyptian slave girl of Sarah. She was the mother of Ishmael.

Haman A powerful official at the court of Xerxes. Esther exposed his plan to kill all the Jews in the Persian Empire.

Hannah The wife of Elkanah and mother of Samuel.

Haran Abraham's brother. He was the father of Lot, Milcah, and Iscah. *Also:* the city where Abraham lived before going to Canaan.

Hebron An ancient city, now in Palestine.

Herod The name of several kings of Judea. Herod the Great was the king visited by the Wise Men. Herod Antipas was the husband of Herodias.

Herodias The second wife of Herod Antipas and the mother of Salome. She told Salome to ask Herod for the head of John the Baptist.

Hezekiah A king of Judah.

Hiram A king of Tyre. He supplied Solomon with wood for the building of the Temple.

Hosea An Israelite prophet. He was the husband of Gomer.

Isaac The son of Abraham and Sarah. He was the father of Jacob and Esau.

Isaiah An Israelite prophet, noted in particular for his prophecies about the Messiah.

Ishmael The son of Abraham and Sarah's slave girl, Hagar.

Israel The name given to Jacob by God. It means "he struggles with God." *Also:* the name given to the Israelites, the twelve tribes descended from Jacob's sons. *Also:* a kingdom formed by these twelve tribes. It later split into the northern kingdom of Israel and the southern kingdom of Judah.

Israelites The tribes descended from the sons of Jacob.

Jacob The second son of Isaac and the brother of Esau. The Israelites are descended from Jacob's sons.

Jael The woman who killed Sisera.

Jairus The father of a girl who was brought back to life by Jesus.

James One of the first disciples of Jesus and one of the twelve apostles. He and his brother John were fishermen. *Also:* the name of another of the twelve apostles. *Also:* a brother of Jesus.

Jehoiada The husband of Jehosheba. He was a high priest who led the revolt against Athaliah.

Jehosheba The wife of Jehoiada and aunt of Joash. She and Jehoiada hid Joash from Athaliah.

Jeremiah An Israelite prophet.

Jericho An ancient city of Palestine. It was the first Canaanite city captured by the Israelites.

Jeroboam The first king of the separate northern kingdom of Israel.

Jerusalem An ancient Canaanite city. King David captured it and made it his capital city.

Jesse The father of King David.

Jesus In Christian belief, the Messiah. He was the son of Mary, who was engaged to Joseph.

Jethro The father-in-law of Moses.

Jezebel The wife of King Ahab of Israel.

Joab A commander of King David's army.

Joash A king of Judah. Protected by his aunt, Jehosheba, he became king after Athaliah.

Job A rich and righteous man who suffered at the hands of Satan.

Jochebed The mother of Aaron, Moses, and Miriam.

John One of the first disciples of Jesus and one of the twelve apostles. He and his brother James were fishermen. He wrote the fourth Gospel and three letters included in the New Testament. *Also:* the author of the book of Revelations. He was thought not to be the apostle John.

John the Baptist The forerunner and baptizer of Jesus.

Jonah A prophet who tried to run away from God and was swallowed by a big fish.

Jonathan A son of King Saul and a friend of David.

Jordan A river that flows between the Sea of Galilee and the Dead Sea.

Joseph Jacob's eleventh son. He was sold into slavery in Egypt by his brothers. *Also:* the husband of Mary, who was the mother of Jesus.

Joshua Moses' successor as leader of the Israelites.

Jotham The youngest of Gideon's seventy sons.

Judah Jacob's fourth son. *Also:* the name of the tribe descended from Judah. *Also:* the southern Israelite kingdom after the time of King Solomon.

Judas Iscariot The disciple who betrayed Jesus.

Judea In Jesus' time, the land to the west of the Jordan River.

Keturah The second wife of Abraham.

Kishon A river in Israel. It flows into the Mediterranean Sea at the modern city of Haifa.

Kohath The father of Amram.

Laban The father of Leah and Rachel and the father-in-law of Jacob.

Lake Galilee Sea of Galilee.

Laodicea A city in the Roman province of Asia (now western Turkey).

Lazarus A diseased beggar in one of Jesus' parables. *Also:* the brother of Mary and Martha whom Jesus raised from the dead.

Leah The elder daughter of Laban. She was Jacob's first wife.

Lebanon A mountain range in what is now the Republic of Lebanon.

Levite A member of the Israelite tribe descended from Levi, Jacob's third son. They acted as assistant priests.

Lot The nephew of Abraham.

Luke An early Christian disciple and a companion of the apostle Paul. He wrote the third Gospel and the Acts of the Apostles.

Manasseh The elder son of Joseph and grandson of Jacob. *Also:* the name of the tribe descended from Manasseh, which occupied land on both the east and west sides of the Jordan River.

Mark An early Christian disciple. He was the author of the second Gospel.

Martha The sister of Mary and Lazarus.

Mary The mother of Jesus. *Also:* the sister of Lazarus and Martha.

Mary Magdalene A woman whom Jesus cured of being possessed by demons.

Matthew One of the first disciples of Jesus and one of the twelve apostles. He was a tax collector and wrote the first Gospel.

Meshach One of three young men who were thrown into a furnace by King Nebuchadnezzar but were saved by God.

Mesopotamia The land between the rivers Tigris and Euphrates (now in eastern Iraq).

Micah An Israelite prophet.

Michal A daughter of King Saul, who became the wife of David.

Midianites People living in Midian, to the east of the northern part of the Red Sea. They were descended from Midian, a son of Abraham.

Miriam The sister of Moses and Aaron.

Moab An ancient kingdom to the east of the Dead Sea. The Moabites were descendants of Lot.

Mordecai The cousin and guardian of Esther.

Moriah The land to which Abraham journeyed to sacrifice Isaac. It is possibly the region in which Jerusalem now stands.

Moses The prophet who led the Israelites out of Egypt and received the Ten Commandments from God.

Mount Ararat A mountain in eastern Turkey. It is traditionally thought to be the place where Noah's Ark landed after the Flood.

Mount Gilboa The scene of a battle between the Israelites and the Philistines, where King Saul and three of his sons were killed.

Mount Nebo The mountain from which Moses looked into Canaan before he died.

Mount of Olives A hill near Jerusalem.

Mount Sinai The mountain in Sinai where Moses received the Ten Commandments.

Nabal The husband of Abigail. He refused to feed David and his soldiers.

Naboth A man who was executed on false charges so that King Ahab could have his vineyard.

Nahor A brother of Abraham.

Naomi The mother-in-law of Ruth.

Nathan A prophet during the reigns of King David and King Solomon.

Nazareth A town in Galilee (now northern Israel), the home of Jesus as he grew up.

Nebuchadnezzar A king of Babylon in the sixth century BC who conquered Jerusalem.

Nehemiah An Israelite leader of the fifth century BC, under whose leadership the walls of Jerusalem were rebuilt.

Nile A river in northwest Africa, around which the Egyptian civilization developed.

Nineveh The ancient capital of Assyria, on the Tigris River (now in northern Iraq).

Noah The man who built a ship in which he, his family, and animals of every species survived the Flood.

Nod The land to which God banished Cain as punishment for killing Abel.

Onesimus The slave of Philemon.

Orpah A Moabite woman, the daughter-in-law of Naomi.

Patmos The island off the southwest coast of modern Turkey, where John received the Revelations.

Paul A Jewish man who was the bitter enemy of the early Christians until he himself became a Christian, after which he actively spread the Christian faith.

Peniel The place where Jacob wrestled with God, thinking He was a man.

Peter Simon Peter.

Pharaoh The title given to the kings of ancient Egypt.

Pharisee A member of a group of Jewish religious teachers who strictly observed Moses' laws.

Philemon The owner of the slave Onesimus, to whom Paul wrote a letter to plead on Onesimus' behalf.

Philip One of the first disciples of Jesus and one of the twelve apostles.

Philistines People who occupied the coastal region of Canaan.

Phinehas The son of Eleazar and grandson of Aaron. He led an attack on the Midianites. *Also:* a son of Eli, the priest at Shiloh, who died when the Philistines captured the Ark of the Covenant.

Phoenicia A country to the north of Israel on the coast of the Mediterranean Sea.

Pontius Pilate The Roman governor of Judea who ordered the execution of Jesus.

Potiphar The Egyptian officer to whom Joseph was sold as a slave.

Promised Land Canaan, the land that God promised he would give to the descendants of Abraham, Isaac, and Jacob.

Queen of Sheba The queen of an ancient kingdom (probably in present-day Yemen) who came to visit Solomon.

Rachel The wife Jacob loved best, the mother of Joseph and Benjamin.

Rahab A Jericho woman who hid Joshua's spies and was spared when the Israelites captured the city.

Rebekah The sister of Laban. She became the wife of Isaac and was the mother of Esau and Jacob.

Red Sea An area of sea between present-day Egypt, Sudan, and Saudi Arabia.

Rehoboam The son of King Solomon who became the first king of Judah.

Reuben The eldest son of Jacob. *Also:* the name of the tribe descended from Reuben.

Ruth A Moabite woman who was the daughter-in-law of Naomi and who married Boaz. She was an ancestor of King David.

Salome The daughter of Herodias. She asked Herod for the head of John the Baptist.

Samaria The capital of the northern kingdom of Israel. *Also:* the region surrounding the city of Samaria, to the west of the Jordan River.

Samaritan An inhabitant of the region of Samaria.

Samson A judge and hero of Israel, famous for his great strength.

Samuel An Israelite prophet. He anointed both Saul and David as kings.

Sarah The wife of Abraham and the mother of Isaac.

Satan The Devil, an evil spirit.

Saul The first king of Israel. *Also:* the original name of the apostle Paul.

Sea of Galilee A large lake in northern Israel.

Sennacherib A king of Assyria who conquered Babylon and Judah.

Shadrach One of three young men who were thrown into a furnace by King Nebuchadnezzar but were saved by God.

Shalmaneser A king of Assyria who conquered the northern kingdom of Israel.

Sheba An ancient kingdom (probably in present-day Yemen).

Shechem A town of ancient Palestine, near the city of Samaria.

Shiloh A town about twenty miles north of Jerusalem.

Silas A Christian who accompanied Paul on his missionary journeys.

Simeon The second son of Jacob. *Also:* the name of the tribe descended from Simeon.

Simon Simon Peter
Also: the name of another of Jesus' first disciples and one of the twelve apostles. *Also:* the name of the man who carried Jesus' cross.

Simon Peter One of the first disciples of Jesus and one of the twelve apostles. He and his brother Andrew were fishermen. Jesus gave Simon the nickname "Peter," which means "rock." He wrote two letters that are included in the New Testament.

Sinai An area of land in northeastern Egypt, at the northern end of the Red Sea.

Sisera The commander of the Canaanite army of King Jabin. He was killed by Jael.

Sodom An ancient city destroyed along with Gomorrah because of its wickedness.

Solomon A king of Israel. He was the son of King David and Bathsheba, and he was famous for his wisdom.

Thaddaeus One of the first disciples of Jesus and one of the twelve apostles.

Thomas One of the first disciples of Jesus, and one of the twelve apostles.

Timothy A companion of the apostle Paul, to whom he wrote two letters that are included in the New Testament.

Tower of Babel The tower built by the people of Babel (or Babylon), which they intended to reach up to Heaven.

Tyre A city on the Mediterranean coast (now located in Lebanon).

Uriah The first husband of Bathsheba. He was an officer in David's army.

Xerxes A king of Persia. He was the husband of Esther.

Zadok A priest who anointed Solomon king.

Zarephath A coastal town, now in Lebanon, where the prophet Elijah brought a widow's son back to life.

Zechariah An Israelite prophet. *Also:* the father of John the Baptist.

Zipporah The daughter of Jethro and the wife of Moses.

Glossary

Acts of the Apostles A book written by Luke, telling the story of the beginnings of the Christian church.

adultery Being unfaithful to a husband or wife.

altar A table or platform where people make offerings to God or a god.

ancestor A person from whom you are descended.

angel A messenger of God, often pictured as a person with a white robe and wings.

anoint To put special oil or holy water on a person's head as part of a ceremony, for example, when they become a king.

apostle A person who believes in something and tells other people about it. Jesus' twelve special disciples are often called the twelve apostles.

archangel A chief angel.

ark The large boat in which Noah, his family, and animals of every species survived the Flood.

Ark of the Covenant A chest containing the two stone tablets on which were written the Ten Commandments.

banish To send someone away from a place as a punishment.

banquet A meal to which many people are invited and where they are offered a lot of food and drinks.

baptism A ceremony in which a person is dipped in or anointed with water, for example, in order to become a member of the Christian church.

bulrush A long-stemmed plant found in rivers and lakes.

centurion An officer in the Roman army.

cherub A type of angel, described in the Bible as a winged creature but now often pictured as a child.

commandment An order; something you are told to do, especially by God.

concubine A woman who is like a man's wife but to whom he is not married.

Covenant Box Ark of the Covenant.

Covenant Chest Ark of the Covenant.

crucifixion The act of crucifying someone.

crucify To put someone to death by nailing or tying their hands and feet to a large wooden cross and leaving them to die.

cupbearer A person who gives wine to a king, often also becoming an important and trusted advisor.

demon An evil spirit.

descendant The opposite of "ancestor." If someone is your ancestor, you are their descendant.

disciple A follower of the teachings of another person. Jesus had many disciples but twelve special ones who were also known as apostles.

dove A white bird of the pigeon family. It was seen as the symbol of peace.

earthenware A type of pottery.

eternal Lasting forever.

Exodus The Israelites' journey out of Egypt under the leadership of Moses.

famine A serious shortage of food affecting a large area of land and many people.

fast A time of deliberately not eating food for religious reasons.

forbidden Not allowed.

fundamental Basic or most important.

Gospel A written record of the life, teachings, and death of Jesus. The word "Gospel" means "good news."

governor A person who rules a country or town on behalf of a king or emperor.

hallowed Treated as holy.

Heaven A place beyond the Earth where God, the angels, and the spirits of good people live after death.

heir A person who receives the money or property of someone who has died.

herdsman A person who looks after large groups of animals such as cows or sheep.

high priest A chief priest.

Holy Spirit God in action in the world.

hostage A person held captive in order to force someone to do what their captor wants.

hypocrite A person who pretends to have moral or religious beliefs that they do not really have.

idol An object or image representing a god or goddess.

inconsolable Impossible to comfort or console.

judge An Israelite leader, often a military leader.

kidnap To take someone away from their family and keep them prisoner somewhere else.

leprosy A serious disease which affects people's skin, hands, feet, and muscles.

locust A large insect like a grasshopper. It flies or crawls in huge groups and feeds on crops, completely destroying them.

Lord's Prayer The prayer that Jesus taught his disciples. It is also known as the Our Father or the Paternoster. It is often said the way it was first written in the seventeenth century, using old words such as "thy" and "art" instead of "your" and "are."

manna The special food that fell from the sky and saved Moses and the Israelites in the desert.

martyr Someone who suffers or dies for something they believe in.

memorial Something built in memory of a person or event.

Messiah The person sent by God to deliver people from evil and bring in a better world. For Christian people, Jesus Christ is the Messiah.

midwife A woman who helps another woman give birth to a baby.

miracle An extraordinary event caused by God.

missionary A person who travels, often to faraway places, to tell people about Jesus.

Nazirite A person whose life is devoted to God. A Nazirite does not cut his hair or drink alcohol.

New Testament The second part of the Bible, containing the teachings of Jesus Christ and the story of the beginnings of the Christian church.

Old Testament The first part of the Bible, telling the story of the creation of the world and the history of the Jewish people.

outcast A person who is forced to live apart from other people.

parable A short and simple story that teaches people a religious or moral lesson.

paradise Heaven.

Passover A Jewish festival that celebrates the Israelites' Exodus from Egypt.

patriarch Any of the great men, such as Abraham and Noah, who were ancestors of the Israelites.

Pentecost A holy day that for Jews comes fifty days after Passover and that for Christians falls on the seventh Sunday after Easter Sunday.

persecution Ill-treatment a person receives because of their nationality, race, beliefs, etc.

pilgrimage A usually long journey to a holy place.

plague A serious illness or disaster that affects many people.

priest A person who leads worship and offers sacrifices.

prodigal Foolishly wasting money.

prophecy A message from God, often describing what is going to happen in the future.

prophet A person who gives people a message from God.

psalm A religious song.

quail A bird that looks like a small chicken.

raven A large black bird of the crow family.

religion Beliefs about God and the worship of God.

resurrection Coming back to life after dying.

revelation A message from God.

ritual Actions performed as part of worship.

Sabbath The day of the week kept for rest and worship. For Jews, it is Saturday, and for most Christians, it is Sunday.

sacrifice To offer something, such as an animal, to God as an act of worship. *Also:* something that is offered in this way.

scribe A teacher of religious law.

scriptures The sacred writings of a religion.

seraph A type of angel.

sermon A speech that teaches religious or moral ideas or explains the meaning of part of the Bible.

Sermon on the Mount One of the first and most important sermons that Jesus delivered to his disciples.

sin Doing something that you know God does not want you to do.

slave Someone who is owned by another person and who must work for that person.

slave driver Someone whose job is to make sure that slaves work hard.

soul A part of a person that lives on after they die.

spirit A person's soul. *Also:* the spirit of God, the Holy Spirit.

synagogue A building where Jews worship.

temptation Wanting to do or have something that you know you should not do or have. *Also:* in the Lord's Prayer, a difficult situation where your faith and courage are put to the test.

Ten Commandments The rules that God gave to Moses, written on stone tablets.

treacherous Dishonestly pretending to be a friend.

treason A serious act of disobedience to a government or an action that brings harm to your country.

tree of life A tree in the Garden of Eden whose fruit would make people live forever.

tree of the knowledge of good and evil A tree in the Garden of Eden whose fruit would give people knowledge about right and wrong.

trespass To enter an area where you are not supposed to be. *Also:* in the Lord's Prayer, to do wrong to someone.

vanity Very great pride.

witchcraft The use of magic spells.

worship To praise and pray to God or the act of doing this.

Index

F

G

L

M

N

O

P

Q

R

S

T

U

V

W

X

Z